OFF TO COLLEGE WITH
KING SOLOMON

A Devotional Handbook for Beginning College Students

D1445903

Pete Charton, Ph.D.

In memory of Luke Samuel Charton, Heaven's child

(2001--2009)

TABLE OF CONTENTS

Preface

Throughout my thirty-five years as a college professor in public education, I enjoyed the privilege of teaching, advising, and counseling thousands of college students from diverse cultures, faiths, and nations. As a Christian, a challenge for me through the years was to respect and appreciate the sometimes very different beliefs and values held by others from divergent faiths (or no faith!) while at the same time quietly seeking to present an unwavering daily testimony to Jesus Christ. Not surprisingly, both successes and failures dot my record in meeting this challenge. In the course of the struggle, frequent journeys to Scripture--often the Proverbs of King Solomon--showed me much about God and how he can fortify professors and students spiritually in the often challenging environment of academia.

Based upon innumerable chat sessions, classroom encounters, weekend retreats, and student conventions, I learned that college students clearly comprise a "people group" possessing special interests and needs. The college years often stand in our collective memories as a unique period in life. Why? Because college is, well, unique! Think about it for a moment. What other institution provides an environment for challenging all established (and often cherished) ideas, encourages continual debate and skepticism over mountainous, as well as miniscule, issues, and places a premium on dissent? What's more, college life inherently embraces change, whether in simple activities like changing class schedules and professors each semester, or in more profound movements such as evolving social and intellectual values. If coping with multiple uncertainties in an academic world is not enough, college students likewise face responsibilities associated with becoming adults in an environment loaded with new friends, financial obligations, athletic and cultural events, parties and social activities, and multiple other distractions. As we shall see throughout this book, college students encountering the excitement and challenge of college can benefit from the wisdom of Scripture, including the wise counsel of King Solomon.

Why base a book about college life on the writings of a man who lived nearly three thousand years ago? Scripture study has accompanied most of my adult life, and frequently when in need of practical, profound advice for coping with life's issues my search would end in consultation with King Solomon. As part of the Old Testament's so-called "wisdom literature," Solomon's books of Proverbs and Ecclesiastes have been particularly useful to me. Sometimes subtle, sometimes blunt, Solomon's statements always get to the point in a hurry. Yes, as translations take us from the classical Hebrew into English we do lose some of the poetry and word associations imbedded in the genius of Solomon's writings, but regardless, the profound content of his writings shines through undimmed. Amazingly, as will become evident in the pages to follow, King Solomon's wisdom adapts readily to issues and needs surrounding college life.

Several objectives guided my writing of this devotional handbook. One objective sought to provide practical advice about college academic life, with scriptural backing, for beginning students making the transition into a college environment. Unfortunately, the time for transitioning is short. For many students, a mere three months or so separates a confident high school senior from a naive college freshman. All at once--usually during the festivities of "Welcome Week"--this college freshman faces numerous far-reaching decisions. These decisions likely will include choosing an academic major (implying a career path), establishing a schedule of classes for the semester, and selecting professors; and, each of these decisions frequently takes place with little, or no, accurate information available to the student. Superimpose over these important decisions the swirling culture of college life, and not surprisingly a significant number of students encounter academic difficulties and serious personal frustrations early in their college experience. Sadly, almost thirty percent of college freshmen will quit school. To make matters worse, struggling students frequently do not know where to turn for help. Thus, as a second objective this book seeks to assist beginning students in decision-making and in understanding the complexities of college life outside of the classroom in order to achieve academic, social, and spiritual success.

The third objective of this book provides spiritual thoughts and Scriptural references of interest to college students who seek answers to life questions. Although a broad spectrum of life's important questions makes its way into this book, trying to address every question held by every individual would be, of course, unfeasible and probably impossible. Alternatively, however, developing a general *process* for approaching all of life's serious issues provides a valuable tool for Christian living. Thus, through the accumulation of individual devotional thoughts presented in this book, I seek to leave the reader with a spiritual, scripturally-based process for gaining guidance and finding answers from God in times of difficulty or challenge. In my view, college--a time of seeking--presents the ideal opportunity for opening spiritual pathways to God and to the wisdom He has promised to those who seek relationship with Him.

Lastly, and underlying this entire book, stands my personal conviction that God's absolute truths provide the keys to unlocking our minds in the search for wisdom, knowledge, and academic success. Of equal importance, an understanding of God's unchanging values can help us in making the sound life-decisions alluded to in the preceding paragraph, such as, choosing a career, selecting a marriage partner, interacting with other people of different faiths or value systems, and many more. Rather than abandoning our faith in God as a barrier to learning and maturing--as college students sometimes do--great anticipation and enthusiasm should prevail because of our access to God's wisdom via our faith!

Christian students constitute a lively and gifted resource for the future of our nation and world. Because a wonderful sample of these students brought such joy, laughter, hope, and fond memories into my years of teaching in higher education, to them I gratefully dedicate this book.

How to Use This Book

You will find *Off to College with King Solomon* a helpful companion as you begin this new chapter in life called "college." The anticipation reaches an end, the imagining gives way to reality. Liberation from the bondage of home rules and regulations has arrived, and now you possess the freedom to make independent choices about nearly everything.

Yet even as we speak of dramatic changes in your life, some words of caution find their place in the discussion. Later in the book we will review some figures regarding the numbers of first-year college students who fall into academic, or other, difficulty; every student should be aware of potential hindrances to success. Therein lies the primary importance of this book: providing practical insights and tips designed to enhance your success academically, socially, and spiritually. Fortunately, Christian students *can* possess a great advantage in higher education; we will discuss this potential, and how to draw from it, later in the book. At this point, I mention the special capabilities of Christian students only to give the following description about the organization and makeup of this book.

Look through the "Table of Contents" at the variety of topics. This is a Biblically-based book of devotions which combines practical information about functioning in a college environment (admittedly from a professor's perspective) with appropriate spiritual guidelines (from God's perspective!). The book consists of ten "units," with each unit subdivided into approximately ten devotions. With the exception of the first unit, this book does not require the reader to proceed in sequence (unless, of course, the reader decides to do so). Rather, the design of the book permits the reader to choose unit topics of current interest or urgency in any order. In other words, the book is very flexible: pick and choose unit topics as you like when a particular need arises and as God leads. Read a unit in part or in total in one sitting; or, read individual devotions on a daily basis. Let your need determine the approach.

However you decide to approach the book, in the end several outcomes should take place. As noted above, you should gain practical advice in adjusting to and successfully dealing with the cultural experience called "college." Further, you should discover a process through Scripture for finding God's help and direction when facing any of life's many challenges, academic or otherwise. Finally, in looking closely at these devotions you may even find some humor woven into the fabric of scholarly conversation!

Let's get started!

Unit One

Maxing-Out Welcome Week

Excitement, fun and fatigue typically characterize the first week of college for new college students. Most institutions of higher learning plan a busy "Welcome Week" (or perhaps a more inventive name characterizes the week at your institution) to kick-off the freshman experience. With noble purpose in mind, nearly all colleges and universities expend considerable money and time providing events designed to draw freshmen into the flow of college life and to assure beginning students about the "rightness" of their decision to attend the institution.

Be glad the chosen college or university cares about your well-being, but try to keep events of the first week in proper perspective. Unfortunately, however noble the intention, Welcome Week sometimes may reinforce popular media images of college life as a time of playing, partying, and "letting go." Rest assured this is not the image the institution means to portray; rather, most often this image develops from misguided students and/or organizations. College should be, and will be, a time of making friends and having fun, but the purpose of college focuses elsewhere (a topic for later discussion). For now, just remember that Welcome Week can become a distortion of reality, a distortion immediately detrimental to your goals and dreams.

The devotions in this unit seek to provide assistance in getting off to a good start in college beginning with Welcome Week. Perhaps surprisingly, how you approach the beginning week may set the tone for your total college experience. Use this week wisely, in addition to having some fun.

COMMIT TO A COMMITMENT

Many are the plans in a man's heart, but it is the Lord's purpose that prevails.
Proverbs 19:21

Two friends of mine, a husband and wife missionary team, long ago made a total commitment of their lives to God. As part of this commitment, Brett and Megan (not their real names) pledged to seek an ever deepening relationship with God and to serve Him completely. I doubt if they could have guessed what God had in store for them as they pledged their lives to Him. Remaining faithful to their commitment through the years, God continues to deploy this missionary couple to exotic (and sometimes dangerous) places. In past assignments, among many responsibilities they interacted with ambassadors and other high government officials; they helped in formulating plans for economic development in countries you would recognize. And they ministered to a significant number of the world's lost and hurting people. By either earthly or heavenly standards, their many accomplishments represent success and fulfillment, and it all began with total commitment.

Before we go any further in this book about achieving success in college, I want you to make an unwavering, total commitment to strive for spiritual growth and for a deepening relationship with God during your days as a college student. Surprised? Don't be! All noteworthy achievements begin with commitment of some kind, and peak academic success for the Christian requires a spiritual connection to the Source (more on this later). So, stop your busy life for a moment, take a deep breath and exhale, humble yourself before God, and then pray a prayer of commitment to seek fellowship with the Master on a daily basis throughout your time as a student. Your times of spiritual renewal each day need not always be lengthy, but they do need to be sincere. Then, and only then, will you be prepared to achieve your full potential as a college student as part of "the Lord's purpose that prevails."

COMMITMENT SQUARED

All hard work brings a profit, but mere talk leads only to poverty.
Proverbs 14:23

In the first devotional of this unit I recommended a commitment to spiritual growth as your first priority in college. Now I am going to suggest a second major commitment for your success as a college student: make academic excellence "job one" for the next four years. Yes, this represents another substantial pledge to yourself and God, and this will mean frequently choosing study time over extracurricular and social activities. But for some good news, these two commitments constitute all of the major commitments required for maximizing your natural abilities as a Christian student. If you need a reminder periodically, remember your two commitments as an equation: commitment x commitment = commitment^2.

Why place such strong emphasis on academics? After all, as long as a Christian student "gets by" in terms of grades won't God take care of everything else regarding the future? Not necessarily. As a Christian, God has a plan for your life, and God intends for you to accomplish something with your life. As part of this purpose, He has brought you to college for preparation. For example, skills such as the ability to reason effectively and to communicate clearly may help to open the doors of your life after graduation from college. In this increasingly complex world, education often becomes a major building block in the life of the Christian who desires to find his place in God's plan.

Let me present one other thought about academic excellence: *grades do matter!* Of course, grades by themselves do not constitute the pinnacle of college life, but they carry great influence if you later decide to go to graduate school (do not laugh, because you never know where God may lead); and potential employers nearly always look graciously upon good grades when hiring new employees. In many of your classes, professors will use grading systems designed to rank statistically the grades for all students in each class. Saying it in a simpler way, you will compete directly with the other students for grades. Thus, make a pledge now to strive for good grades as part of your commitment to academic excellence.

PENCIL ME IN

The plans of the diligent lead to profit, as surely as haste leads to poverty.
Proverbs 21:5

Yogi Berra, former great Major League baseball player and "philosopher," once observed: "You've got to be careful if you don't know where you're going because you might not get there." Applied to college life, Yogi's observation hits the center of a problem shared by many college students, namely, a lack of planning toward graduation. In other words, nearly all students desire to graduate from college, but many often fail to develop a clear avenue toward accomplishing the goal. This lack of planning nearly always results in lost time, additional expense, and delayed graduation.

As an incoming freshman experiencing Welcome Week, you probably will not be able to outline a firm route to graduation in terms of required courses and scheduling--few students can at this point (although some academic departments may be able to furnish a suggested four-year schedule for those choosing their major). Happily, you can do just fine for the first year or so by selecting classes that apply to just about every academic major, classes such as English composition and math. Eventually, however, you will need to select a major subject area and to formulate a detailed semester-by-semester plan leading to graduation; generally, the sooner you know your academic direction the better. (In Unit Four of this book we will talk more about selecting a major and long-range planning toward graduation.)

For now, however, begin looking ahead to the time when you will decide on your academic major, and perhaps a career, by keeping alert for subjects of exceptional interest and by praying persistently for God's leadership to the eventual correct choice. As our Bible verse states, "The plans of the diligent lead to profit...."

LIGHTEN YOUR LOAD

Listen to advice and accept instruction, and in the end you will be wise.
Proverbs 19:20

Many visiting college football teams schedule a "walk-through" of the opponent's stadium the day before a game. What does a walk-through accomplish? It allows players unfamiliar with the stadium to walk the playing field, to examine the playing field surface for imperfections or uneven spots, to imagine the crowd and noise level, and to project themselves carrying-out their assignments on the way to victory. In many respects, the walk-through provides a "virtual" experience for the players as they mentally see themselves competing in the game.

In a similar way, the first college semester should provide a walk through experience which previews college life and the challenges of higher education. As such, listen to this no-nonsense advice about scheduling that you, your parents, and especially your college advisor will question. But it is sound advice based on years of personal experience advising and observing students: *enroll in no more than twelve to fourteen credit hours the first semester and take half of these hours in easier courses.* Just make certain these easier courses will apply to most majors, usually as "elective" hours. (Scan the college catalogue for interesting course titles; for example, my son enjoyed "A History of Rock N' Roll Music" his first semester.)

Your college advisor may become uneasy about a "decaffeinated" schedule, but give it consideration. Why? Because the first semester likely will involve significant emotional, social, and intellectual adjustments on your part, and often these adjustments negatively impact grades. Leaving a familiar cultural setting (home, high school, friends) in exchange for a new and very different culture (college) provides challenges. Give yourself a break and lighten-up the first semester. After that, you will have plenty of time plus the confidence to take-on the tough classes and schedules. As King Solomon noted, "in the end you will be wise."

"GPS" YOUR SCHEDULE

Apply your heart to instruction and your ears to words of knowledge.
Proverbs 23:12

The Global Positioning System (GPS) consists of twenty-four orbiting satellites, in six orbital planes, continually transmitting signals for earth-bound reception. (Whew!) A great technological achievement, GPS helps ships navigate seas, surveyors find boundary lines, geologists monitor changes in the earth, wildlife managers track animal migrations, farmers apply fertilizer for better crop yields, and many, many other useful applications. What exactly does GPS accomplish so wonderfully? Location, location, location! GPS lets us determine very accurately and quickly the location of nearly anything on earth!

No, I am not suggesting that you rush to buy a GPS unit in order to find your way around campus. However, I do recommend taking a couple of hours to "prayer walk" the campus and become oriented to the buildings and facilities that will be important to your life as a student. Walk through your schedule of classes in order to determine locations and how much time will be needed to make the journey from class to class (plan on arriving at least five minutes before each class begins). On very large campuses you may need to factor in bus schedules or making the journey via bicycle. Arriving late to classes the first day, as some beginning students inevitably do, will not cultivate favor with professors. As you walk through the schedule, pray for the professors who will teach you, for fellow students with whom you will interact, and for God to give you wisdom and understanding. Finally, mark precisely each building location on a campus map and make any necessary notes to enable an easy return to each place.

Becoming familiar with the campus before classes begin will return valuable dividends in the form of self-confidence and making good first impressions with both students and professors.

BURNING BRIDGES

Let your eyes look straight ahead, fix your gaze directly before you.
Proverbs 4:25

Long ago in the struggle for Texas' independence, the men of General Sam Houston's weary army found themselves seemingly trapped near the San Jacinto River by a larger and better equipped enemy. Courageously, General Houston ordered the burning of a bridge, the only escape route for either army. In doing so, the Texans had no alternative but to "look straight ahead...." and engage their enemy. The famous Battle of San Jacinto, won by the Texans, lasted only about twenty minutes and forever changed the course of Texas history.

Like Sam Houston's army, nearly all college students who go away from home will face an enemy. We call this insidious enemy "homesickness." Whether homesickness hits in the first week or later, it must be addressed squarely; if not, it has the capacity to destroy your college experience. This enemy reveals itself in a variety of ways, from depression and complaining to friends and parents about conditions at the institution, to going home regularly, to constantly thinking of home, and so forth.

Although no quick-fix applies to everyone, the following thoughts may help in overcoming the enemy. First, remember why you chose to attend this institution; the reasons likely remain valid. Further, realize that you are becoming an adult and this homesickness is a normal part of the transition. Fond memories of home and friends will remain, but you cannot re-create the past. Finally, remember God's presence in your life and how intensely He wants success for you.

It's time to look forward and not backward. It's time to burn some bridges.

LONELY IN THE CROWD

A man of many companions may come to ruin, but there is a friend who sticks closer than a brother.

Proverbs 18:24

Even an apostle could experience loneliness! It's true. Read the Apostle Paul's comments in 2 Timothy, Chapter 4, for example. Writing from a depressing Roman prison in this very personal letter to his young colleague, Paul acknowledges both the nearness of his coming execution and how much he longed for a visit from two friends, Timothy and Mark. Yet in the face of loneliness and uncertainty, the apostle remained decidedly positive in his faith and outlook, thereby setting an example for us to follow.

For the college student, loneliness often walks hand-in-hand with homesickness; in fact, one easily may trigger the other. Whether loneliness comes sooner, or later, like homesickness it needs to be dealt with proactively. What did Paul do to confront loneliness? He remained positive in his thinking, and he reached out to others. You should do likewise. For example, force yourself to seek-out a new friend by visiting campus religious organizations like Baptist Student Ministries (BSM), the Wesley Foundation, and numerous others. These groups nearly always provide a place to hang-out and to make new friends, friends who will provide positive influences in your life. Some of my fondest memories as a professor derive from the merriment provided by Christian students when I served as faculty sponsor for their organization.

Additionally, investigate campus interest groups for one that coincides with your favorite hobby or activity. On most campuses clubs exist for a variety of interests including hiking, photography, environmental action groups, and you name it. These organizations carry the obvious advantage of bringing together students who possess similar interests.

Remember, making friends normally takes place one at a time, so exercise patience. As your list of friends grows, you likely will find the one King Solomon described: "a friend who sticks closer than a brother."

PRESENT TENSE, PLEASE!

Do not boast about tomorrow, for you do not know what a day may bring forth.
Proverbs 27:1

Jules Verne, famous science fiction author in the late 1800's, based the outcome of his wonderful book *Around the World in Eighty Days* (written in 1873 and more recently given the Hollywood touch in movie form) on a simple geographic fact. As seen in the journey of Phileas Fogg, the book's central character, a traveler moving eastward in a complete journey around the earth would gain one full day on the calendar. Yet, even though Phileas Fogg "gained time" by traveling eastward, gaining time proved only a trick of the calendar. He added no actual time to his life, nor did he somehow experience living in future time. Rather, of necessity the adventuresome Mr. Fogg continued to live each minute of every hour of every day *in the present.* With fewer words, King Solomon served-up the same truth about living in the present in Proverbs 27:1. We must live in the present. Life provides no other options!

Why discuss this obvious point in the context of college life? Because all too often students fall into the "futuring" trap to the detriment of their mental health, academic progress, and joy. We need to make a distinction between *planning* for the future and *worrying* about the future. Planning nearly always provides positive outcomes, whether the planning encompasses activities for a day, week, or semester. Everyone wishing for success in life needs to develop effective planning skills and habits. However, once the plans reach completion do not continually dwell on them. Continuing to focus on future assignments and responsibilities often triggers a mental paralysis destined to provide only negative results. Instead of worrying and constantly re-playing "all the things I have to do," shift your focus to the present and what can be done today in accomplishing goals.

Remember, plan for the future, but live in the present. You will become a better, happier student!

STICKY NOTES

Folly delights a man who lacks judgment, but a man of understanding keeps a straight course.

Proverbs 15:21

Hopefully our prior discussions reinforce the idea that Welcome Week can provide substantial benefits to the entering college student who chooses to use this time wisely. Although we have addressed a number of important issues, a few more items require attention as you prepare for the start of classes.

For example, buy necessary books and materials, check technology connections and requirements, purchase athletic tickets, secure a parking permit, look at several churches you might wish to attend, and so forth. These items by themselves do not represent major obstacles; however, after classes begin, collectively these can become tiresome distractions.

Finally, begin learning to organize your life in a formal way. Sticky notes and I go back many years; anyone passing by my desk will see loads of yellow "tags" reminding me of things I need to accomplish by a certain date. Sticky notes, or their modern communication equivalents, work well in personal time management; or, a common day-planner available at most bookstores provides another good alternative. Whatever method you select, from the first day of classes make a habit of recording all important assignments, due dates, and special responsibilities for each class. Then, revisit your "calendar" every day. Most professors fail to display warmth and compassion when students miss an announced deadline, for whatever the reason!

For the student who "keeps a straight course...." toward the goal of academic achievement, college life provides fun and fulfillment. By always meeting due-dates, a student earns the privilege and freedom to socialize and enjoy the best of college life.

GOING FOR THE GOLD

...choose knowledge rather than the finest gold.
Proverbs 8:10b

When I hear someone say "going for the gold," an expression coined during intense Olympic competitions to describe athletes headed for victory and a gold medal, memories of past Olympics immediately come to mind. In my appraisal, no Olympic track star ever better exemplified the full aura of "going for the gold" than did Michael Johnson in the 1996 Olympics. Johnson, former Baylor University track star and arguably America's best sprinter of the modern era (or maybe ever), won gold medals in both the 200 meter and 400 meter events. In doing so, he set a world record in the 200 and an Olympic record in the 400. Wow!

In training for competition, sprinters expend large amounts of time and effort developing techniques for efficiently springing from the starting blocks, because the first few steps "out of the blocks" often mean the difference between winning and losing. Michael Johnson bursting from the starting blocks looked like a giant spring uncoiling with unbelievable power and speed. In a similar but figurative sense, how you move "out of the blocks" the first week and first semester of college likely will hold great importance in the running of your "race," too.

As Welcome Week comes to an end, your commitments to God and to academic excellence should serve as strong motivations for learning; as well, hopefully you will have taken care of many of the practical matters addressed under previous headings in this unit. Thus, now you can approach the beginning of classes with enthusiasm and confidence. In beginning your race toward a successful college career, hear King Solomon praise knowledge as an intangible prize more important than gold.

Run your race well!

Unit Two

On Being A Freshman Without Being "A Freshman"

Nearly any worthwhile enterprise requires discarding preconceived ideas and adjusting to new ones. Such is the case with college life. In particular, college classes usually conform to certain unwritten rules of behavior and participation. Unfortunately, these standards often do not become apparent to an uninformed freshman until after a "stumble" has occurred.

This unit will help in avoiding some of the more common freshman *faux pas* in the classroom. Although every possible slip-up cannot be listed, we at least can create a helpful set of examples for demonstrating different types of unflattering behavior in a classroom setting. With a modest amount of attention, you quickly will learn to evaluate possible actions before undertaking them.

Students logically want to appear competent, prepared, and mature to their peers and professors. Thus, let's look at some ways of overcoming "freshmanitis."

KNOCKING ON OPPORTUNITY'S DOOR

Stop listening to instruction, my son, and you will stray from the words of knowledge.
Proverbs 19:27

Francis Bacon, former great English philosopher and statesman, once observed: "A wise man will make more opportunities than he finds." Not only do these brief words express a truth borne out by life experiences for many of us in the "older generation," but Bacon's words likewise infer a solid life-principle for the college student: view every class and class-meeting as an opportunity to learn!

Why state the obvious, especially when "learning" constitutes the central reason for going to college? Because many freshmen (and unfortunately even advanced students, too) seemingly want to place "learning" into their own narrowly defined comfort zone. Frequently, as a college professor I heard students voice the following unsolicited complaints about some class or professor: "the professor is boring"; "the class is not in my major, and I do not like the subject matter"; "I never will use this information"; "the class is not important in today's world," and numerous others. Frankly, these complaints, and others like them, are largely irrelevant and display some degree of academic immaturity.

The grand purpose of an undergraduate, liberal arts college curriculum exists to expose a student to a broad array of subject areas, ways of reasoning, and general approaches to life. Some subject areas, professors, and possible career paths you will like; others you will not. *However, you can learn something of value--often a lot--from every class and every professor regardless of the subject matter and the personality!* This, of course, takes us right back to the purpose of undergraduate, liberal arts education.

By achieving entrance to college you have created an important opportunity for your future. Enhance this achievement by approaching every day and every class as a new opportunity to grow intellectually. To paraphrase King Solomon, if you listen to your professors, you will become knowledgeable!

R-E-S-P-E-C-T

A man of knowledge uses words with restraint, and a man of understanding is even-tempered.
Proverbs 17:27

The late comedian and actor Rodney Dangerfield often voiced his signature quote: "I don't get no respect." Coming from him the expression always seemed humorous. If a survey were taken of college professors, I imagine many would agree with Rodney Dangerfield about themselves.

Presumably most students do not intend to show disrespect for their professors, but very often actions speak louder than intentions. Let's be clear. When I speak of respect for your professors, I am not talking about adoration, reverential regard, paying homage, or even agreement; rather, I mean displaying basic courtesies to the professor, your classmates, and in a broader sense, to the academic process.

Under several topics in this unit we will look at some specific behaviors on the "disrespectful" list. For now, however, two general ideas about professors should become firmly implanted in your thinking; and if you are unsure about a contemplated action or comment involving a professor, weigh the possible action in light of these two ideas beforehand. First, professors are human, and they respond emotionally to events and words like everyone else (although many professors have learned to mask their outward reactions). Ask yourself, "How would I respond if our roles were reversed?" If the answer is unsettling or not clear, you might want to rethink the intended action or statement.

Second, in spite of stereotypes sometimes portrayed by the entertainment media, professors usually rank highly in intelligence, knowledge, and understanding student behavior. Further, professors live for learning, teaching, and research. As a college student, you tread on their "turf." Most professors readily recognize immature or unacceptable behavior; likewise, sarcasm and "brown-nosing" hit discordant notes. By contrast, sincere interest in the course subject matter can warm even the coldest professorial heart.

Professors can help your future in a variety of ways, some of which we will mention under other headings. Treat professors with respect, and they will hold you in high regard.

RIGHT THINGS

To do what is right and just is more acceptable to the Lord than sacrifice.
Proverbs 21:3

Throughout the Scriptures God reveals His expectation of those who follow Him to do good things for others in life's daily events. "To do what is right and just...." in a scriptural sense often applies to many different settings and activities. For example, in the New Testament we see Jesus actively healing the sick, blind, and infirm. He even "cured" the dead (see Matthew 8-9)! Yet, in a very different context, King Solomon tells us to take care of the needs of our enemies (Proverbs 25:21). The chief principle coming from these and many other similar passages is clear: as believers, we have a broad obligation to be considerate and to act honorably toward those with whom we interact.

Just how does this principle of doing "what is right and just...." apply to a college class? Probably in many ways, but, importantly, it means that you as a student should not detract from the professor's teaching or management of the class nor interfere with your classmates' opportunity to learn. For example, most good students arrive at least five or ten minutes before a class begins in order to arrange materials and themselves for learning. Your late arrival to class distracts both professor and students, thus interfering with teaching and learning. If you must enter late, enter quietly and sit as close to the entry door as possible. Perpetual tardiness constitutes a sure means of creating a negative image with both professors and classmates!

Remember to think of your classmates: they have made significant commitments of time and money in order to attend college. Remember your professors: each class represents a portion of their life's work, backed by preparation and planning. Remember yourself: you want to learn, and you want to create a positive image with others.

Finally, remember the Scriptures: "do what is right and just...." in the classroom, and you will gain the admiration of the professors and other students, as well as the blessing of God.

HOT SEATS

A discerning man keeps wisdom in view, but a fool's eyes wander to the ends of the earth.

Proverbs 17:24

As a teacher of historical geology, I sometimes asked the question of various groups: "How long is a long time?" The answers normally varied by age and status. Working adults frequently told me with a smile, "A long time is to retirement." Scholars solemnly presented "the age of the universe" as their yardstick of time; and elementary school children frequently spoke about the great age of grandparents representing "a long time." For college freshmen, based upon my in-class observations of the "fidget-factor," comatose expressions, discreet checking of cell phones for text messages, and wandering eyes, a "long time" constitutes about thirty minutes!

Professors learn to "read" college classes. When a student becomes inattentive, even in a large class, the professor usually soon notices the change. Typically, inattentiveness occurs with underperforming students; not surprisingly, better students rarely seem to lose focus during the duration of a class-meeting. Isn't this similar to the observation made by King Solomon in the verse quoted above?

Fortunately, discipline and planning can overcome loss of focus in the classroom. As an example, one easy way to increase your attention span and academic performance involves sitting as close to the front of the room or lecture hall as possible. In a well-known study[1], researchers found better performance by students seated near the front because they interacted with the teacher both verbally and visually more than those students seated toward the back. Numerous other published studies contain similar findings. Thus, help yourself by arriving early for class, choosing a seat near the front, and mentally focusing on the subject matter for the day. By doing so, you will join with King Solomon as a discerning person who "keeps wisdom in view...."

---

[1] Adams, R.S. & B.J.Biddle. *Realities of Teaching: Explorations with Video Tape.* New York: Holt, Rinehart & Winston, 1970.

COMMON SENSE

The wise inherit honor, but fools he holds up to shame.
Proverbs 3:35

Desirable conduct in the college classroom frequently results from subdued actions as opposed to showy ones. As such, "respect" for professors and classmates usually appears in quiet, understated ways. On the other hand, some student acts in the classroom throw subtlety out the window. Often, these actions seem so inappropriate as to border on ridiculous. From my college days through my years as a professor, I watched intelligent, well-meaning students let logic and judgment slip away as they made conspicuous behavioral errors in the classroom.

Take a look at the following common sense list of "do-nots" and brief accompanying comments.

1. Do not use a smart phone to text, email, surf the internet, or anything else during class time. Rather, turn off the device and hide it.

2. Do not talk, interact with other students, or fall asleep during class. This behavior insults the professor.

3. Do not work on assignments for another class during the present class or read newspapers and other materials. The professor nearly always knows and reacts negatively.

4. Do not take food or drink to class, and *never* open candy or other snack food wrappers during class lectures. A volcano eruption and a wrapper opening during class possess equivalent noise levels, or so it seems.

Remember the purpose of this unit: to help avoid breaches of classroom etiquette, and to help you, a freshman, behave in a manner which gains the respect of your professors and classmates. Exercise in-class awareness and judgment, mixed with a little discipline, and in return you will gain the admiration of others.

TALK THE TALK

A word aptly spoken is like apples of gold in settings of silver.
Proverbs 25:11

Peter, the great apostle, sometimes irritated Jesus by saying the wrong thing. For a sample, look at John 13 where Peter's refusal to let Jesus wash his feet earned a sharp rebuke. Ouch! Saying the right thing at the right time may turn the direction of debates, ease tensions in an argument, or comfort people steeped in sadness. Saying the wrong thing, however, invariably makes a situation worse and embarrasses the speaker (and maybe others).

Learning when to speak and when to keep silent in a college classroom requires experience and maturity as a student. Generally, as a new college student you will benefit by exercising caution before plunging into an open classroom debate (which the professor likely has encouraged for his purposes). Let's be clear. This advice refers only to open-ended discussions requiring opinions and conclusions by class members on subjects you may not have researched or considered fully (for example, a social issue). This advice does not relate to direct questions from the professor about assignments or course content, which you must try to answer.

Effective speaking and reasoning skills comprise two of the most valuable assets a college student can develop for later professional success in nearly any field or occupation. Freshman enthusiasm for exercising these abilities may prompt speaking out. Yet, your total college experience will last at least four or five years; thus, exercise good judgment and restrain your enthusiasm for a time. Once you see and understand the character of classroom debates, you will be better prepared to join in the verbal jousting.

Who knows? You may possess a talent for public debate, a potentially useful clue in the search for a career path. Perhaps your words will seem "like apples of gold in settings of silver."

QUESTION MARKS

I, wisdom, dwell together with prudence; I possess knowledge and direction.
Proverbs 8:12

A professor friend of mine at the University of Illinois frequently reminded graduate students under his supervision: "Asking the right question is the beginning point of solving any problem." In other words, only by asking the right question about a problem can you discover the right answer. Absorb his thought for a moment, then memorize this insight and make part of your life--all of your life! Remarkably, in one brief observation based upon the experiences of a lifetime, this professor has handed you the key to problem solving in every area of life. Applied to spiritual pursuits, asking a good question helps us find appropriate scripture for guidance; applied to academics, proper questions provide insight into complex problems. In life, asking thoughtful questions unlocks the doors to success. Learning to ask the appropriate question at the appropriate time takes effort and focus, but the payoff yields great rewards.

Just as asking the right question reveals reflection and understanding of a problem, asking the wrong question portrays a lack of thought and perception. Putting it another way and perhaps more to the point, asking poorly considered questions in class can make a student look especially foolish to classmates and the professor. This being the case, every student as part of their educational goals should make a determined effort to master the skill of asking sound questions.

Luckily, asking questions about subject matter (such as history or biology) provides a legitimate, "safe" opening for developing the ability to ask perceptive questions. Even a poorly asked question in a subject matter context likely will be welcomed by the professor. On the other hand, exercise caution regarding ill-planned general or personal questions (such as those presented in the next devotion). Finally, ask God for help in learning how to develop this vital skill. This skill carries such great importance in the life of a Christian that ultimately only God's wisdom can teach us how to do it well.

DON'T ASK

A prudent man keeps his knowledge to himself, but the heart of fools blurts out folly.

Proverbs 12:23

For modern professors, asking questions constitutes an important means of leading students to ponder difficult issues and problems. But the roots of this teaching technique extend to an ancient origin dating at least as far back as Socrates and other ancient Greek scholars. Likewise Jesus, the Master Teacher, frequently presented his listeners with questions in order to make a point. For example, in Luke 14:1-6, Jesus asked two questions of the scribes and Pharisees; these elite of Jewish society suddenly became tongue-tied. Some of Jesus' parables actually began with questions (see Luke 15).

Students, too, should ask questions in class. Most professors enjoy solid, insightful questions from students; good questions indicate a student's interest and commitment to the course. On the other hand, students sometimes ask off-the-wall questions lacking in substance or thought-- professors often share these around the coffee pot in the faculty lounge! My personal favorite came when a student asked me in class if I would raise my hand each time I said something of importance, in order to aid his note-taking! I did not agree to this arrangement.

The questions below represent the common kinds of questions *not* to ask your professors. Scraping your fingernails on a chalk board likely would bring a kinder professorial response!

1. "I lost my pen. Do you have something I can write with?" (Possessing proper materials comes under your responsibilities as a student. Period.)

2. "I had to miss the last class session. Did I miss anything important?" (Of course you did! Further, you just told the professor that most of his classes possess little value.) Of all the foolish questions often asked by students, most professors would rank this as number one.

Be wise. Think first. Don't ask.

ANTSY

Go to the ant...consider its ways and be wise!
Proverbs 6:6

Of all God's creatures, ants surely comprise the best role models for beginning college students. Why? Because most ant species daily demonstrate energy, inventiveness, and determination for survival, exactly the traits necessary for success in college and life. Even with ants, "preparation" results from directing these traits toward specific goals or purposes. For example, a rain forest ant nicknamed the "doormaker ant" (*Stenamma alas*) builds slightly raised nest entrances with a pebble positioned nearby. When predator insects come snooping, the ant simply pulls the pebble over the opening, thereby creating an impenetrable stone door. Further, these ants dig many false doorways and tunnels leading to empty nests in order to confuse marauding enemies. How's that for preparation!

Like the ants, students need to prepare vigorously. Class preparation should begin with a thorough awareness and understanding of the course syllabus. A well-constructed syllabus takes time and effort to create because it reflects the professor's vision for the class, and it represents a contract between the professor and students for a particular course and term. As such, the syllabus likely will contain all major assignments (such as term papers, projects, and the like), due dates, and examination schedules. Extract this information for each course, write it on a calendar, and then check the calendar *every day* during the semester. Missing due dates guarantees making a poor impression with your professors and classmates. The syllabus also should present an overview of the course, course readings, and important goals and themes of the course. Carefully ponder the syllabus for each course as a first step in preparing to do well.

In the next topic we will extend our discussion of academic "preparation." For now, however, simply remember the ants. Proper preparation by them-- and you-- requires hard work and determination. Resolve with King Solomon and the ants to prepare wisely in order to achieve success!

PREPARE YE

Lazy hands make a man poor, but diligent hands bring wealth.
Proverbs 10:4

My wife and I enjoy watching collegiate women's basketball, and we marvel at the competitiveness, enthusiasm, and skill of so many talented athletes. Competition between women's teams from different colleges and universities comprise some of the greatest rivalries in the world of sports. But of all the players and athletic programs across the United States, not one developed without consistent, well-directed preparation.

Likewise, in order to enhance academic achievement consistent preparation must take place. Preparation always precedes success in the classroom! What kinds of things do we include under the heading of "preparation?" The list may vary, but some items show up for nearly every class. For example, assigned readings in your text or other sources should be done prior to every class meeting in order to understand class discussions and to ask questions about difficult concepts. Further, written assignments, term papers and projects, and class presentations should receive early and regular attention prior to their due dates (that calendar thing, again). Hint: Begin the preceding activities *on the day they are assigned*; doing so will encourage early completion (plus your stress level will remain lower as the required dates approach). Finally, and this one takes discipline, after every class lecture rewrite and organize your lecture notes before the class meets again. Among other benefits, organizing your notes this way makes studying for exams much easier.

Place preparation for classes at the center--not the perimeter-- of your college world. Further, remember the following old adage because its truth endures both for great athletes and great scholars: "Unspectacular preparation produces spectacular results." Amen!

TEAMWORK

One man gives freely, yet gains even more; another withholds unduly, but comes to poverty.
Proverbs 11:24

Many human activities require teamwork, but none demands it more intensely than high-altitude winter mountaineering. Immersed in national pride and almost-fanatical determination, renowned Polish mountaineers conquer the world's great mountains under the harshest of winter conditions in a sport developed largely by their forefathers. Of the world's fourteen peaks with altitudes over 8,000 meters (about 26,247 feet), the hardy Polish adventurers have successfully climbed eight in winter under the harshest conditions imaginable. Temperatures below -40° C, nearly hurricane-force winds, and blinding snow storms commonly beset the intrepid mountaineers, but still they strive to enshrine their legacy on the world's highest peaks. Where death and mission failure may come abruptly, success (and survival) demands the highest level of teamwork.

College demands teamwork, too. Students frequently must share responsibilities with classmates as researchers on assigned projects, coworkers in science labs, or members of study groups. In each of these settings, cooperation--teamwork--will determine success or failure. Usually, the most successful teams succeed through the participation of *all* team members. The least successful groups often rely on one or two people in the group to perform most of the work. From the professor's view, the final research paper or presentation to the class nearly always indicates the level of effort by each team member. Significantly, team members often express hard attitudes toward other team members who do not contribute meaningfully to "the cause." Beware!

As a freshman, gain the respect of your peers and professors by showing a willingness to work and to help your classmates. In other words, accept responsibility and carry it through to completion. To paraphrase the wise observation of King Solomon: As a student, give freely to your classmates and receive even more in return!

BEND, DON'T BREAK

Whoever gives heed to instruction prospers, and blessed is he who trusts the Lord.

Proverbs 16:20

The Bible showcases failure! Look at some of the Biblical heroes and read their stories. Moses murdered an Egyptian; King David arranged the death of a trusted soldier in the midst of an adulterous affair with the soldier's wife; Jonah ran from God; and, the Apostle Paul killed Christians. Do you need more examples? How about Peter's denial of Jesus in the face of promises to the contrary; or, how about the time the prophet Elijah ran in fear from Queen Jezebel to hide in the desert? We can find many other examples of failure by God's chosen representatives. Yet, the stories never end with failure; rather, failure ends with success!

Why, then, does failure rear its dismal head in so many Biblical accounts pertaining to Scriptural "giants"? Time and again the Bible pronounces the same verdict: God requires humility and repentance of every person before they become worthy to carry His purpose forward. No exceptions! Failure constitutes a common way for God to bring us to our knees before Him. Then, at this point our relationship with God strengthens, our faith takes hold, and we go forth again with humble determination and confidence.

As a student, events may bring failure into your life. Perhaps you will perform poorly on an exam or a term paper, or perhaps you will make one of the embarrassing freshman mistakes outlined in this unit. Perhaps you will experience difficulty with an entire course. When events become negative, follow our Biblical predecessors and bend your knees before God, asking for forgiveness, mercy, wisdom, and understanding.

Above all, do not panic or quit. To the contrary, like the heroes of Scripture, learn from your mistakes and work diligently in faith to improve. Remember, God hears, and your professors listen; so talk to both of them as part of the improvement process. Bend your knees; don't break your faith.

TAKING CARE OF BUSINESS

The heart of the discerning acquires knowledge; the ears of the wise seek it out.
Proverbs 18:15

Throughout this unit we wove our way through a variety of devotional thoughts designed to help your transition from high school student to successful college freshman. With moderate effort and focus, you should learn quickly regarding the "do's and don'ts" of classroom behavior. Keep in mind that nearly every entering college student will go through a rather hurried maturing process during the first semester, and nearly all will make mistakes of one type or another. However, with the opening of the second semester, most of these same students will enter their classes with a much more confident and scholarly attitude. To point out the obvious, the quicker you develop a "feel" for the college environment, the quicker you will begin to feel a sense of anticipation and purpose in your classes and in college life generally. When this happens, looking back at the past will assume a level of unimportance, and you will begin to see promise in the future. At this point you will have become a "college student" in the fullest sense.

As we close this second unit, refresh your prior commitments to God and to yourself for spiritual growth and academic excellence. Place these important commitments at the center of your college life, and then fit all the other activities associated with college around these. In other words, start good life habits early and watch your successes multiply. In doing so, "taking care of business" will become a daily reality in your life.

Unit Three

Time(ly) Management

Effective time management often presents a great challenge for inexperienced college students. In fact, how a student manages time may mean the difference between success and failure. College life consists of several levels of "do" categories. For example, the "must do" category includes eating, sleeping, and maintaining a positive bank account. The "need to do" list encompasses worshipping, studying, writing term papers, paying parking tickets, and so forth. The "rather do" list frequently encircles the largest selection of activities like sunbathing, hanging-out in the student lounge, playing computer or video games, and dating. Choosing among "do" categories and prioritizing daily schedules comprise critical choices for success in college (and for success in professional life after college!).

ACT (yes, those folks who construct bothersome tests) compiles data about many aspects of college. Based upon records dating to the early 1980's from four-year private and public colleges and universities in the United States, disturbingly, about thirty percent of freshmen nationwide will not enroll for their sophomore year! (The drop-out numbers run even higher for two-year institutions.) [2] Look at your classmates and friends and imagine that at least three out of every ten will not attend college after the freshman year. The reasons often given for dropping-out of college comprise a long list of misfortunes: grades, finances, homesickness, illness in the family, dislike of academic life, and others. Regardless of the reasons, a large number of students drop-out and relinquish their dreams of a college degree.

From my observations through the years, nearly all successful students possess an ability to manage time efficiently; weak students rarely possess this skill. Ineffective time management frequently leads to frustration, falling behind in class work, and serious discouragement to the point that factors like finances and other causes listed in the preceding paragraph may tip the balance toward quitting. Therefore, Unit Three seeks to provide students with effective, timely management skills for succeeding in college. College success depends more upon time management, study skills, discipline, and determination than on brain power. If you have been accepted to a college or university, you possess the mental ability to become a college graduate. Thus, let's now learn about a set of skills designed to make it happen.

---

[2] Source: ACT Institutional Data File, 2001

THE GIFT OF TIME

There is a time for everything, and a season for every activity under heaven....

Ecclesiastes 3:1

I once heard a captivating speaker liken our lives to the wheels on an automobile. Balanced wheels run smoothly, but, a wheel out of balance begins to vibrate and thump along, eventually ruining the tire if not corrected. Like the wheels, each of us needs balance in our life in order to experience joyful, successful living. This means our work, worship, recreation, extra-curricular activities, and social life need to be chosen and ordered with purpose. Failure to manage time efficiently in personal and professional settings usually brings undesirable results; in college life, poor time management may translate to high stress levels, sleepless nights, and lower grades.

Face this truth: twenty-four hours comprise each day, and every individual chooses how to use those twenty-four hours. In other words, every person possesses the same amount of time; but how people deploy the time depends upon personal choices. Thus, the often uttered "I don't have time ...." makes a weak excuse for most situations. Actually, you and I "own" as much time as anyone else; but, perhaps our skills in allocating time need improvement. Fortunately, with determination and discipline (and maybe some help from your college's counseling office) any college student can learn to manage time more efficiently.

Look at time as the Bible does. The Scriptures make it clear that both life and time belong to God. Further, by giving us life, God necessarily gives us time, too. Just as God intends for us to use our lives productively for Him, He intends for us to use our time productively for Him. Ecclesiastes 3:1 begins with this simple, elegant statement from Solomon: "There is a time for everything...." Thus, in God's way we can learn to balance our lives in order to accomplish all God has planned for us.

"Time" represents a precious gift from God. Honor God in return by using your time wisely.

FREEDOM ISN'T

He who heeds discipline shows the way to life....
Proverbs 10:17a

Investing in the stock market presents a magnificent opportunity for individuals to participate in national and international business and commerce. With a dance of the fingers on a computer keyboard, any person (assuming adequate financial resources) can invest in nearly any industry in nearly any country in the world. Just think of the freedom! Companies in Australia, China, India, Russia, Brazil, and the USA--the list seems endless--await stock market investment dollars. Thus, with study and diligence, you possess the world beneath your fingers as well as the opportunity to become wealthy. Of course, this wonderful freedom to invest worldwide comes with a sobering downside, in that, the possibility of losing wealth from your investments looms large. Whether from unwise stock choices or from uncontrollable events, this freedom to buy stock offers a distinct opportunity to fail. In failure or success, you, and you alone, must assume all responsibility for the choices.

An unmistakable parallel exists between investing in the stock market and "investing" in a college education. Like the stock market, college life presents a large array of choices at every level. For example, the larger choices include an academic major, friends, and activities to name a very few. Smaller choices, such as attending classes, occur on a daily basis; however, these daily choices may significantly impact the chances for academic success, too. Think particularly about time allocation. You may use your time wisely or foolishly each day, but, like the stock market, you, and you alone, must assume all responsibility for the choices.

As the prodigal son of Scripture discovered the hard way (Luke 15:11-32), freedom really never comes free; every freedom and every resulting choice carry the related burdens of responsibility and consequences. Learn to use your time wisely and begin paving the way to success. Let discipline show you "the way to life...."

BE STILL

The fear of the Lord is the beginning of wisdom, and knowledge of the Holy One is understanding.

Proverbs 9:10

The golfing world displays many behavioral traits peculiar to the sport. To me (the perpetual duffer), none exceeds "addressing the ball" in terms of importance--and humor. "Addressing the ball" refers to the moments before the swing begins; during this time, the golfer seeks to put mind and body together for a successful stroke of the ball. Further, no two golfers address the ball in quite the same way. Some golfers wiggle from head to toe, often multiple times, while others stand like stone; some hit the ball immediately, whereas others fall into deep meditation. Some golfers repeat bodily rituals worthy of prehistoric holy men, and others seem to improvise. Yet, for all the differences, the purpose of the "address" remains the same for every golfer: to focus on the dimpled surface of a small white ball in order to hit it squarely and accurately.

In our hurried world, God speaks directly to his followers through his Word regarding many subjects, including time management. Clearly, we find the first step in successfully organizing our time consists, not of checking our calendar, but of checking our focus--our focus on God. In other words, our beginning point of wise time management should be a *spiritual* one. In Psalm 46:10 God tells us bluntly, "Be still and know that I am God...." Does this get your attention? It should, because in this verse God gives us a lesson on how to "address" Him. God desires our total focus on Him, that he might lead us daily throughout life.

Effective time management, then, becomes an issue of our commitment (that word again!) and our faith. "Being still" with God each day resets our mind and puts us in sync with God's will and purpose. Thus, if you lack the habit of meeting with God every day, preferably early in the day, learn to do so and see how many aspects of life begin to change, including your skills in time management. King Solomon said it best: "The fear of the Lord is the beginning of wisdom...."

TIME CHUNKS

He has made everything beautiful in its time. He has also set eternity in the hearts of men; yet they cannot fathom what God has done from beginning to end.

Ecclesiastes 3:11

Admired evangelist Billy Graham once described each person's time on earth as "a little chunk of eternity."[3] Truly, when compared to astronomers' current calculations for the age of the universe at twelve to fourteen billion years (also a small portion of eternity!), our human time "chunks" look small indeed. Yet even though our lives fill but a brief portion of the cosmic calendar, Scripture repeatedly defines the importance of an individual's time on earth. For example, Ephesians 5:16 urges Christians to act wisely "making the most of every opportunity...." in God's eyes.

How, exactly, do we please God with our time? A guiding principle for *all* of a Christian's life pertains to obedience. A Christian needs sensitivity to God's leadership and willingness to act accordingly. More specifically, however, Matthew 25:31-46 provides one of the most startling insights in all of Scripture regarding God's final evaluation standards for Christians at the judgment seat of Christ. As we read through these verses, we do not see mention of great achievement, fame, or wealth. Rather, we read about helping the hungry, sick, lonely, and those in prison. Imagine the world impact if all Christians everywhere took this passage seriously!

As a college student, learn to give your time by assisting others as God has commanded. Most college campuses offer numerous, on-going opportunities to serve others. Helping others does not necessarily mean working through campus Christian groups or area churches, but these organizations nearly always present immediate access to worthwhile projects. In addition, these Christian organizations and churches usually attract energetic, bright young people who could become your cherished, life-long friends. Make the most of your chunk of eternity by serving others in Jesus' name.

---

[3] Graham, Billy. *Day-By-Day with Billy Graham.* Ed. Joan Winmill Brown. Minneapolis, MN: World Wide Publications, 1976.

DISTRACTIONS

In his heart a man plans his course, but the Lord determines his steps.
Proverbs 16:9

Throughout my life, I have watched a parade of important movements, issues, and charismatic leaders stir people to action both in the United States and in other countries. Wars, political controversies, international epidemics, and social issues regularly provided the motivations for protests, demonstrations, relief efforts, acts of compassion, and other notable responses. Some of these eye-catching events possessed a nobleness about them; others seemed less than worthwhile. Either way, today a majority of these formerly intense issues and leaders merit modest mention, if any, in history books.

While I attended graduate school at Michigan State University in the late 1960's, the Viet Nam War was raging, and our country edged closer and closer toward civil, social, and legal chaos. Civil disobedience, created largely by college-aged young people and their energetic leaders, dominated the headlines, and multitudes of students left college to protest the war and other social issues. Sadly, many of these students never returned to complete their college degrees. Did the war constitute an important national issue? Yes. Did students possess a legitimate right to express their feelings? Yes (although unfortunately their means of expression sometimes violated civil behavior and the law). Did involvement in these issues justify quitting college? In most cases I think not, because careers and futures died as a result.

A significant part of wise time management involves putting first things first. Certainly, issues need the involvement of intelligent, concerned citizens. However, God gave you the task of "college," and until this mission reaches completion, finishing your education should remain the primary goal. Your time to make a difference in this world will come, but first *prepare* for the task. Issues and charismatic leaders come and they go, but God's purpose always remains.

DIVERSIONS

He who works his land will have abundant food, but he who chases fantasies lacks judgment.

Proverbs 12:11

Picturing someone busier than a President, Prime Minister, or other high-ranking government official challenges the imagination. Each day the tasks and responsibilities shouldered by these national leaders boggles our minds and makes us wonder how they manage the pressures of office. Not to over simplify, but one ingredient shared by many successful leaders may surprise you: nearly all possessed a personal passion for activities far-removed from their leadership roles. For example, Winston Churchill discovered painting as a young man and went on to produce over five hundred works. Dwight Eisenhower loved to paint and cook; Sandra Day O'Connor enjoyed exercise classes and whitewater rafting. Dr. Condoleeza Rice, an accomplished pianist, met regularly with a small group of outstanding amateur musicians to play chamber music. For past national and international leaders, the list of diversions includes many varied activities.

Diversions (in college known as "extracurricular activities") may help students escape suffocating pressures brought about by homework, exams, and term papers. Why? Because diversions reset our minds and emotions thus enabling us to freshly approach our responsibilities. In short, diversions can be good *if* kept in proper perspective. Diversions may take the form of simple activities such as hiking and swimming, or more involved activities like Christian organizations, marching band, political action groups, or even sororities and fraternities. Whatever you choose, make certain you look forward to participating in the activity!

Finally, recognize the time commitment required for each of these extracurricular activities. To believe that you can participate in a multitude of organizations (as you may have done in high school) represents a giant step toward the "fantasies" decried in our Scripture reading. Select one or two regular extracurricular involvements as an aid to academic success and good mental health. King Solomon would be proud of your judgment!

ANTICIPATION

The prudent see danger and take refuge, but the simple keep going and suffer for it.
Proverbs 27:12

Music came easily for my father. Gifted with a beautiful tenor voice and a genius intellect, he could perform, write, and direct music at any level. Following a brief period as a college math professor and then Army service in World War II, Dad devoted his life to church music ministry. Although the music gene largely by-passed me, I did "volunteer" to sing in many of his choirs through the years where I learned about music. Frequently, Dad instructed his choirs to "anticipate" musically--whether the downbeat, the tempo, the emotion of the piece, or other features; at all times, he encouraged his musicians to think ahead. At some point I finally grasped the musical importance of "anticipation."

In fact, as time progressed I began to see a much broader application of "anticipation." Nearly all successful people in whatever field or enterprise--music, sports, business, medicine, or you name it--strive to foresee the future and then plan accordingly. Apparently, King Solomon recognized the value of "anticipation," too!

So much about success in college revolves around anticipation and managing time. For example, watch your professors early in the term for patterns regarding their interests and biases in subject matter; this can help in preparing for tests. When performing class assignments, identify the issues or concepts central to potential class discussions. Then, mentally prepare your viewpoints or responses *beforehand* in order to avoid the "What, who me?" appearance if asked a question in class.

As a college student, learn to anticipate coming events, and where necessary, to allocate appropriate amounts of time in your schedule for completion. Thus, with term papers or projects always anticipate the maximum (*not the minimum!*) difficulty and time of completion. Hint: Begin your project research on the day of announcement; avoid last minute finishes which nearly always compromise quality, cost a lot of sleep, and interfere with completing other assignments. Become a happier, better student: anticipate, execute, relax!

DUE DILIGENCE

The sluggard craves and gets nothing, but the desires of the diligent are fully satisfied.

Proverbs 13:4

What do restaurants, motels, department stores, discount stores, grocery stores, and many other enterprises share in common? Among other things, these businesses employ college students. Unlike bygone times when college tuition and related costs came to smaller, more manageable totals, working to earn money for college stands as a reality for many students today. In the face of soaring expenses, determined students still seem able to find ways of paying for college. In fact, I would describe the efforts by many of my former students in this regard as "heroic"!

If by necessity or by choice you intend to hold a job during your time as a college student, bear in mind several considerations. First, effective time management dictates a shortage of hours to engage in extra-curricular college activities. You can enjoy your college experience, but be prepared to miss some, or many, events because of work schedules and study requirements. Second, depending upon your major, you may need to reduce the number of credit hours taken, at least in some semesters. For example, classes with attached laboratory requirements such as chemistry, biology, or geology require significantly more time as compared to non-lab classes. Third, create your semester schedules wisely. You must allow sufficient travel time to reach class from work, and you must arrange classes around the work schedule. Even though professors silently may be cheering for you as a "working" student, most professors view repeated class tardiness or absences with a cold attitude. In fact, the word "Arctic" immediately comes to mind!

Would you like to hear some good news about college students who work? Recent studies indicate that employed students tend to use their time more wisely than their non-working counterparts, resulting in higher grades. Yes, you read correctly; working students tend to make higher grades! King Solomon noticed a similar truth nearly three thousand years ago: "the desires of the diligent are fully satisfied."

REST STOPS

Of making many books there is no end, and much study wearies the body.
Ecclesiastes 12:12b

Wilma Rudolf possessed the elements of greatness. Blessed with star athleticism, she exuded grace, dignity, humility, and intelligence. Many Tennessee youngsters, including me, revered this African-American star of the 1960 Rome Olympics. Born in Clarksville, Tennessee, near my home of Nashville, the local newspapers constantly wrote of her many victories in track, especially her three gold medals in Rome (a first for any female Olympian). "Poetry in motion" did not begin to describe her fluid running style.

To watch Wilma Rudolf run, however, masked a surprisingly difficult childhood for this twentieth of twenty-two children in the Rudolf family. At four years old, Wilma became ill with polio, a serious and often deadly disease, resulting in an immobile left leg. Although told by her doctors that she would never walk without leg braces, a supportive family and a determined mother instilled in her the competitiveness of a champion to overcome the impossible. As they say, "the rest is history" in this story of courage.

According to a newspaper article I once read, Wilma Rudolf possessed an amazing ability to "zone out," meaning she could clear her mind of surrounding stress or worry and fall asleep almost immediately. This same article quoted her as saying she could even "cat nap" while *standing* if a conversation or situation became boring! Why take these quick naps? She said the naps re-energized her to meet the needs of a demanding schedule.

Let's learn a lesson regarding sleep from this great track star. College provides a demanding and often tiring environment. Studies, events, and social demands regularly conspire with one another to render sleep a scarcity. During times of sleep deprivation and stress, learn to take a few minutes each day for a brief "rest stop." You will discover that a little sleep goes a long way toward restoring mental and physical efficiency. After all, as King Solomon noted, "much study wearies the body."

CONTEXT

There is no wisdom, no insight, no plan that can succeed against the Lord.
Proverbs 21:30

As we come to the end of our time management unit, perform some self-evaluation. What strengths in time management do you possess? What weaknesses stand out as points for improvement? Remember, effective time management requires practice to perfect it and discipline to incorporate it into everyday life. Fortunately, college life makes a great training ground for mastery of time management skills.

As we have stressed in various ways in this unit, by developing strong time management skills in college, these skills will accompany you throughout life. All successful people, regardless of profession or endeavor, have learned to organize their time. Yet, as important as these skills are to successful living, for the Christian time management must be seen in a much broader context. Look again at our Scripture verse given above. At first glance this verse might seem out of place in a discussion of time management. But once more, King Solomon very plainly puts a simple truth in front of us.

Ask yourself this question: "Am I honestly seeking God's will and leadership in my life each day and then managing my time accordingly?" If you answer "no" to the question, based upon our Scripture verse you run the risk of choosing directions that run counter to God's purpose; if so, these plans face difficulty from the start. On the other hand, the flip side of our Bible verse means that a "yes" answer to the question brings the reasonable expectation of *many* good outcomes while living in God's plan for your life.

God wishes successful living for you, and King Solomon provides directions toward that end. For the highest level of time management and timely management, place your life in the context of God's will and see what successes come your way. God promises!

Unit Four

Major Considerations

Of the important considerations forced upon all college students, none ranks higher than choice of an academic "major." Why? Because selection of an academic major touches several life-directing issues whose outcomes likely will influence career choices, future economic status, life style, eventual place of residence, and service to God to name a few. Thus, choosing a major--in other words, a concentration of courses in an academic discipline such as economics, geography, mathematics, political science or one of many others--should merit serious thought and prayer prior to making the decision.

In this unit, we will examine some of the important steps for a Christian to take in selecting a major field of study. If you truly wish to find God's will for your life, identifying the right academic major can be a crucial step in positioning your life for His service. Discovering the appropriate direction of study may come slowly for some students, producing frustration and impatience; for other students, the answers may appear more quickly after only a brief time of seeking. Just remember, God provides answers based upon His calendar, not ours.

Unfortunately, no single piece of advice or procedure fits the needs of every student in their search for God's direction. Saying it another way, no pat answers exist; rather, students must consider a group of common variables. The Lord will mix and shuffle these variables differently for each person according to His purpose. Your job through prayer, Scripture study, reason, and listening is to sift through the variables and to watch God's plan emerge during the search. Eventually when the search ends with God's revelation, think of the exhilaration (and relief) you will feel in knowing that God spoke to you about your life!

Remain faithful. He will.

PURPOSE?

Many are the plans in a man's heart, but it is the Lord's purpose that prevails.
Proverbs 19:21

"God has a plan for your life!" Do you believe this statement? Take a moment or two and ponder not only the statement but the multiple implications that go with it. Does the possibility of a divine plan for each believer's life really exist? If so, how do we sign-up for it? These questions should provoke serious thought and self-examination throughout this unit. Further, at some point seeking God's purpose will lead the college student to the serious task of choosing an appropriate academic "major."

But first, does God hold a plan for your life? A positive answer to the question means a Christian needs to search vigorously for this life "compass" from God, for obvious reasons. A negative answer means life pretty much becomes a series of personal choices directed toward a self-constructed outcome. So, what do the Scriptures tell us? The Bible provides an emphatic "yes" to this question in many forms and places in its pages. Jeremiah 29:11 issues an often quoted guarantee on this subject: "For I know the plans I have for you," declares the Lord, "plans to prosper you and not to harm you, plans to give you hope and a future." God's intention is clear. Thus, here and in numerous other references the Bible tells of a God-designed plan for each individual believer. Just think, God took the time to map a life plan for you and for me!

For most Christian students, finding God's will requires a personal journey of discovery through extensive prayer, Bible study, patience, and other actions discussed in subsequent devotional topics in this unit. If Christians seek diligently in the confidence of Scripture, God will reveal the answers. Make the journey and trust King Solomon's words for successful living in the fullest sense: "it is the Lord's purpose that prevails."

ADJUSTMENTS

A man's steps are directed by the Lord. How then can anyone understand his own way?

Proverbs 20:24

Henry Blackaby and Claude King produced a widely recognized, deeply inspirational book titled *Experiencing God.*[4] One crucial concept in this scripturally-based book emphasized an invitation offered by God to believers for joining Him in His work, based upon the Biblical requirement for followers of Christ to adjust their lives in order to accomplish God's purpose. Through the years in my talks with many Christian students about their direction and purpose in life, nearly all expressed a genuine desire to discover and accomplish God's will. However, the large majority approached God exactly backwards, and because their approach was wrong, their search for God's plan frequently produced disappointing results.

How can we approach God in precisely the wrong manner? By graciously and sincerely inviting God to join us where we are! Do you see the subtle, yet profound, difference between this statement and the Biblical approach described in the first paragraph? We should join God, and not vice versa. A Christian who is unwilling to adjust life to meet God's purposes faces a life of frustration.

Do you remember my missionary friends, Brett and Megan, who were described in the first unit of this book? Everyday, they ask for God's guidance in meeting Him. By their accounting, this eagerness for adjusting their daily life to God's purpose regularly sharpens awareness of God's broader plan for their ministry. As the authors of *Experiencing God* said: "What you plan to do for God is not important. What He plans to do where you are is very important."

To discover God's purpose for you, and by extension to help in choosing an academic major compatible with God's plan, put first things first. Seek to find where God wants to meet with you each day and adjust your life accordingly. In meeting with God regularly, you will find your steps "directed by the Lord...."

---

[4] Blackaby, Henry T. & Claude V. King. *Experiencing God.* Nashville: LifeWay Press, 1990.

INVENTORY TIME

Remove the dross from the silver, and out comes material for the silversmith.
Proverbs 25:4

Lu Xiaomin, born in 1970 into China's largest Muslim community, seemed an unlikely candidate for greatness as a Christian. As recounted by author David Aikman in *Jesus in Beijing*[5], an insightful book about Christianity in China, Xiaomin dropped out of middle school because of illness. After permanently leaving school, she helped her family as an agricultural laborer. One day while picking cotton, a Christian aunt led nineteen year-old Xiaomin to faith in Jesus; immediately, she began attending a house-church fellowship. One evening after a worship service, Xiaomin tried to fall asleep but could not because an unknown song moved in her mind. The next day this shy girl sang her newly composed song to another girl, who, in turn, sang the song for her Christian parents. From this tiny but momentous beginning, God began presenting Xiaomin's musical talents to China. Although neither Xiaomin nor anyone in her family knew music in any formal way, by 2002 at the age of thirty-two, this quiet young woman had penned nearly 900 (!) songs of faith. Recognized as one of the most influential Christians in China today, Xiaomin continues to write, minister, and use her talent as God directs her.

Why discuss Xiaomin? Because she beautifully illustrates two concepts. First, God gives talents to each person; and, developing these talents is part of our job as Christians. Second, God wants individuals to use these talents for Him. In case of doubt, God rarely leads people away from their talents. Thus, by identifying academic talents you may move a step closer to selecting an appropriate direction of study in college.

"Do I work well with numbers?" "Do I possess a knack for learning languages?" "Does the realm of science intrigue me?" "Do I thrive on public interaction?" While pondering the future, ask yourself questions like these. Then, give yourself realistic answers. Only by "removing the dross...." (eliminating the unlikely possibilities) can you begin to identify the Master Silversmith's design. Take inventory of your talents today.

---

[5] Aikman, David. *Jesus in Bejing*. Washington, DC: Regnery Publishing, Inc., 2006.

PASSION

A happy heart makes the face cheerful, but heartache crushes the spirit.
Proverbs 15:13

Christine majored in psychology, an interesting subject area with few direct avenues to employment (without graduate degrees). Thus, like many college students Christine's goals lacked definition. However, Christine enjoyed the study of psychology and refused to be deterred from her chosen major. Sometime following her junior year, she felt a tug toward elementary education which, in retrospect, she identifies as "God's hand on me." Today, after earning a masters degree in education, Christine teaches second grade children and loves it. Further, her training in psychology prepared her in an unanticipated way for understanding and meeting the needs of children and parents of children with special mental, physical, and learning needs. Christine followed her passion (the study of psychology); later, God took control and adapted her specialized training to His purpose.

Previously, we discussed the very real need for taking inventory of talents as a help in selecting an academic major. However, enumerating our talents may not yield all of the information necessary for making the right choice, because enthusiasm and motivation--your passions-- will play important roles in your success, too. If your talents and passions do not parallel one another, trying to balance them in choosing a major may prove challenging. With Christian students, prayer combined with Scripture searches should occupy high priority in the total analysis. Further, most college counseling offices offer an array of free or inexpensive tests designed to uncover student abilities and interests, which may produce both surprising and useful results.

In any case, I can assure you of one truth: If you experience prolonged dissatisfaction in your chosen major, you likely will not achieve either joy or success. Refuse to dwell upon money, fame, or the urging of parents and loved ones in selecting a major. Rather, follow your passions! King Solomon reminds us: "A happy heart makes the face cheerful...."

CAREER MYTHS

A simple man believes anything, but a prudent man gives thought to his steps.

Proverbs 14:15

As a boy, playing baseball added purpose to my life. Until high school graduation, most summers I would play on at least three teams. Pictures of famous Major League players lined the walls of my room at home, and, I boldly told people of my dream to play in the Big Leagues. When college baseball scholarships came my way, I owned the world; I now possessed a real reason to attend college! Then, after two years in college when professional baseball made offers, life changed again. I signed a contract to pitch for the Boston Red Sox, and a short time later I stood on the mound in Fenway Park pitching against those great American League players of the early 1960's. I loved baseball with all my heart, and, for me a dream career had become reality. Wow! Could life get any better?

During my rookie season in the Major Leagues, a strange realization occurred: I found I did not like the life associated with professional baseball. I continued to love playing baseball, but I did not like living it. Boredom became the persistent enemy. Sitting in hotel lobbies and movie theaters waiting to play the day's game, day after day, became unpleasant; and living out of a suitcase while traveling to one large city after another from March to October played havoc with my general attitude. Am I condemning professional baseball with these statements? No, because for many players, professional baseball represents a coveted career; for me, however, it did not fit well. I simply had made poor assumptions. When a shoulder injury and subsequent surgery ended my brief baseball career, I returned to college with an entirely different perspective regarding the role of academics in my life, so much so, that I decided to become a college professor!

As you search for an appropriate college major, inevitably you will touch upon likely career paths tied to various academic choices. Look very hard at the lifestyles and commitments associated with different careers and try to make few assumptions. Remember, "a prudent man [person] gives thought to his steps."

CAREER REALITY

All hard work brings a profit, but mere talk leads only to poverty.
Proverbs 14:23

The beautiful Colorado River, while racing over 1450 miles from the Rocky Mountains to the deserts of the American Southwest, traverses some of the most spectacular landscapes in the world, including the Grand Canyon. Many years ago, the river possessed the ominous descriptive title "a river of no return." Westward the river supposedly disappeared underground and travelers on the water vanished in an unpleasant death. Fear, not fact, ruled. But, in 1869 Major John Wesley Powell, a geologist and wounded Civil War veteran, launched boats carrying an exploration party down the Colorado. Enduring a dangerous trip in risky wooden boats, the intrepid explorers eventually passed successfully down the violent river waters, including those in the Grand Canyon, thus disproving the dire reputation of "a river of no return." Today, river rafting through the Grand Canyon provides a daily major attraction for tourists.

In the preceding piece ("CAREER MYTHS") we noted the risks associated with making poor assumptions. In the paragraph above, *inaccurate information* produced some very silly conclusions about the Colorado River. As a college student, becoming a "truth sleuth" should constitute a primary goal for you, particularly in important life-decisions such as selecting an academic major and eventually a career. Do not be misled by movie and televisions depictions (where characters go to work but rarely work), ill-informed guidance counselors, or acquaintances who seek to live vicariously through you.

On the positive side, pray. Then, talk with professors in fields of interest; most will want to help you. Visit the counseling offices of your college or university; frequently counselors possess printed information and points of contact for different professions. Finally, and of paramount importance, find people working in areas of interest to you; from these people you should be able to obtain firsthand information about majors and careers. Uncovering a direction in life rarely comes easily. As King Solomon implies, work hard toward finding reliable information; "mere talk..." probably will not help much.

THINK IN NEW WAYS

Trust in the Lord with all your heart and lean not on your own understanding; in all your ways acknowledge him, and he will make your paths straight.
Proverbs 3:5-6

Katie, our older daughter, teaches ESOL (English Speakers of Other Languages) to elementary students, most of whom arrived in the United States only recently. Beginning her career as a history teacher, she quickly found limited numbers of job-openings in this popular field. Thus, in pursuing a master's degree Katie decided to look for a more employable field of study. The answer for her came in the field of ESOL, a profession experiencing tremendous demand growth as the rest of the world seeks to learn English. Thus, God led her to discover a means of using her passion (history) with a highly employable emerging field of study (ESOL). Today, Katie teaches her ESOL students about America's history!

Let's mention another aspect of how God leads receptive people to his service. As a Christian, Katie always wanted to minister to disadvantaged, hurting people. Guess what? God led her to the right place through ESOL. Although still a young teacher, Katie could fill a book with her stories of ministry to these children--everything from obtaining eye glasses and other medical remedies for the children, to assisting frightened parents, and to uncovering cases of child abuse. God spoke, and Katie listened.

In searching for a college major, try thinking in new ways. In other words, look beyond the conventional majors and see what you find. Some lesser-known fields of study can be very interesting, offering excellent job and career prospects. Your college or university catalogue provides a great starting point for discovery. Further, think for a moment about the hottest fields of study today; many, such as network systems and data communications analysts, computer application software engineers, and data base administrators did not exist a few years ago. New fields continually emerge.

Finally, wrap your searches in prayer and openness to God's leading. Long ago, King Solomon found the secret: Trust the Lord with all your heart...."

WILLINGNESS

The lamp of the Lord searches the spirit of man; it searches out his inmost being.

Proverbs 20:27

"He too saved Israel." So ends one of two verses in Scripture detailing the life of a mysterious Biblical hero named Shamgar, a man who saved his country during a time of great peril (Judges 3:31; 5:6). What else does Scripture tell us about this little-known hero? He slew six hundred marauding Philistines with an oxgoad (a long stick with a spoke on one end and a chisel-shaped blade on the other for herding oxen). Further, he became one of the judges of Israel during a time when Israel frequently faced destruction from surrounding enemies. Biblical historians speculate that he probably tended and drove oxen for a living, thus suggesting a poor man from a lower tier of society. Clearly, though, Shamgar possessed courage, faith, and a willingness to serve God, both as a warrior and a judge of Israel.

Throughout this unit, discussions have focused on various aspects of selecting a major field of study. Hopefully, by now a mental checklist of considerations occupies part of your thought process on this important topic. But, as Shamgar demonstrates, our checklist is not quite complete. Shamgar adds *willingness* to our checklist, a new, vital requirement. Suppose Shamgar had refused to obey God's directions to him. Can you imagine the results? Would God have called someone else? Maybe. Or perhaps Shamgar's failure to respond to God's leadership would have brought defeat and suffering to Israel. An absence of willingness to follow God's plan may produce serious consequences!

When the "lamp of the Lord" searches your spirit, what will He find? Will He find a student who possess a willingness to step forward on faith? Will he find a student who believes "success" reaches completion only in accomplishing God's will? Decide today to learn what God can do with your life. In other words, remember Shamgar, deliverer of Israel and keeper of oxen!

MAJOR CHANGES

For a man's ways are in full view of the Lord, and He examines all his paths.
Proverbs 5:21

Our son, Ross, selected the University of Montana for his college education. Soon after arriving there for his freshman year, he announced his intention to major in business education. Somewhat surprised at his choice and the suddenness of the selection, I asked about his motives in choosing this particular major. With his typical honesty and humor, I learned that business education constituted one of two majors at the university not requiring a foreign language. Apparently memories of high school Latin proved too much for him to bear! Yet amid my profound skepticism about his motives, Ross tenaciously pursued his degree, which included a life-changing involvement in ROTC. To our great pleasure, Ross graduated in exactly four years, a feat accomplished by a minority of American college students. Today, Major Ross Charton regularly uses his training in education and business while serving with distinction in the United States military.

The U.S. Department of Education's National Center for Education Statistics (NCES) estimates that only about 40% of college students in America graduate in four years. Further, the average length of stay for graduates of public and private institutions as calculated by NCES approaches five years. These widely quoted figures give pause for thought, because, unless you plan and execute carefully, college may develop into a longer, more expensive venture than originally planned. Although the reasons for delayed graduation may be multiple, changing majors frequently enters the picture. Over half of all college students change majors at least once, according to The National Research Center for College and University Admissions.

Changing majors necessarily translates into lost time and added expense. Delay declaring a major as long as prudent, and as a freshman and sophomore take as many generally required courses as possible. (Note: Some majors such as pre-med may not allow this flexibility.) Then, when academic preferences finally come into focus, you can declare a major with confidence, knowing your ways "are in full view of the Lord."

PATIENCE

Commit to the Lord whatever you do, and your plans will succeed.
Proverbs 16:3

The Great Wall of China, one of the spectacular engineering projects in human history, remains today as a monument to the estimated three million Chinese who died in its construction. Stretching for over 4,160 miles, the roughly twenty-five feet tall and twenty feet wide barrier sought to protect the Chinese heartland from invaders. As such, the Great Wall's history reflects the larger aspects of Chinese history including wars, diplomacy, and the passing of ruling dynasties. How important was the Great Wall? During the peak years of the Ming Dynasty, for example, over one million soldiers guarded one section of the structure. Perhaps most amazing of all, the Chinese worked on building, and in some cases rebuilding, the earth, stone, and brick fortification for over twenty-two centuries. This defines "patience"!

Sometimes discovering a proper direction in life--in this case identifying an academic major--reminds us of the patience needed in building the Great Wall of China. For many students, identifying a major requires time and experience in order to give God opportunity to lead to a point of understanding. Do not rush the process, and do not expect to see all of God's plan unfold at one instant. Sometimes God may work this way, but usually God reveals parts of His will on a step by step basis. Remember, too, in this part of your life as a student you need an academic major, not a career. Yes, your major and your career likely will join one another, but it does not always work this smoothly. Identify the major first, and God eventually will lead you to the career.

In pursuing this unit we have examined a variety of considerations connected with choosing a major field of study. In blending all of these considerations, exercise patience--patience with yourself and with God. Above all, pray and develop relationship with God in order to hear God's answers. Sometimes, God speaks very quietly through a simple feeling or inclination. King Solomon reminds us of a wonderful Biblical promise regarding issues we commit to the Lord: "your plans will succeed."

Unit Five

It's Academic

For many entering students, college classes represent a dramatic departure from high school. For example, classes do not meet as often each week, assignments frequently require more thought and effort, and attendance requirements may not exist. Further, and perhaps least understood (and least appreciated), students may encounter from both the professor and other students a continuous stream of questions whose answers rely more upon reasoning than on memory. And to the discomfort of many, the questions may lack clear answers or applications, while at the same time challenging a student's core values and beliefs. So, what gives? Why the question-and-answer sessions and not more "teaching" of concrete information and ideas?

To begin with, the answers lie in an understanding of the purposes of a college education. Some would say the purpose of a college education is to provide information, and to an extent, a college education certainly does this. But as important as information may be, many in higher education would contend that leading students to think critically, reason accurately, articulate ideas effectively, and locate reliable data represent more valuable objectives for the long run, since "information" soon becomes obsolete. As a means of accomplishing each of these educational goals, higher education normally relies on a group of loosely defined procedures sometimes referred to as the "academic process." The particulars of academic process may vary from professor to professor and from institution to institution. Yet the heart of the process everywhere centers on examining issues openly and fairly in an effort to discover the truth, and a significant part of the process requires questions and answers, challenges and responses, and defense of conclusions.

We will say more about academic process in the following pages. For now, however, do not retreat from the academic process; rather, seek to understand the objectives and applications of the process and use them to your advantage. Again--amazingly--King Solomon already seems to have addressed our topic!

EYE-OPENER

Blessed is the man who finds wisdom, the man who gains understanding.
Proverbs 3:13

"Open my eyes, that I may see glimpses of truth Thou hast for me; Place in my hands the wonderful key that shall unclasp and set me free...."

So begins an old, well-known hymn with this profound plea for understanding--a plea that should be the intense desire of every Christian college student! As we shall see in this unit, God, through King Solomon, spoke many times about His authorship of wisdom and understanding. Ultimately, as the old hymn infers, truth of any type belongs to God.

In college life, the way of seeking wisdom, understanding, and the truth normally comes through the "academic process," an approach to learning we referred to in the introductory comments to this unit. To repeat, if done properly, the academic process theoretically clears the way for open and unbiased examination of any issue or idea appropriate to the class subject matter. The process respects all viewpoints while challenging all viewpoints. This means questions, answers, rebuttals, and more questions by both the professor and students at times will dominate the class; it also means you need to prepare thoroughly for every class meeting in order to participate effectively. The faster you grasp the philosophy behind this approach to learning, the faster you will appreciate the profound ways the academic process can sharpen your abilities of reasoning, thinking critically, researching information, and articulating thoughts, clearly some of the most important products of higher education.

Let the academic process "open your eyes" to "glimpses of truth" that God has for you. In today's Scripture reference, God assures us of blessings when we obtain wisdom and understanding. Further, in Proverbs 4:7 God *commands* us to obtain wisdom. Take God's promise of blessing and His command to obtain wisdom seriously--King Solomon did. In fact, invite God to accompany you each day throughout your college career. Can you think of a better way to begin a lifetime of learning and understanding than to have the Author of wisdom at your side? I cannot.

GOD, THE REAL NUMBER

By wisdom the Lord laid the earth's foundations, by understanding He set the heavens in place...

Proverbs 3:19

Albert Einstein, renowned mathematician and scholar, seemed determined to deny the existence of God. But try as he might, Einstein's own mathematical genius forced him down the path to enlightenment about God and creation. Perhaps Einstein's greatest achievement came with the publishing of his equations of general relativity in 1915 and 1916. To astronomers these equations possess profound implications regarding the origin of the universe. In a rather long series of steps based upon follow-up research by other great scientists, notably astronomer Edwin Hubble, Einstein reluctantly admitted proving the existence of God through his equations. Today, many modern scientists agree with Einstein's conclusions regarding the existence of a God who created the universe. Think of it: mathematical proof of the existence of God!

Of course, Einstein's "discovery" would have amused King Solomon (and many other Biblical characters) who knew of God's existence nearly 3,000 years ago. However, in a more direct context, knowing of Einstein's mathematical proof and subsequent belief regarding the existence of God as Creator should fortify the confidence of every Christian student. As you study, consider, and debate new--and sometimes controversial--ideas, rest your confidence and trust in the "proven" God. Whether it be in debates as part of the academic process, in discussions with fellow students who may or may not be believers, or in your own reflective moments, enjoy the quiet assurance of knowing that God exists and He speaks truth to you through His Word.

Try to imagine the difficulty of college life without this assurance.

PLAYING IN THE DARK

I know that everything God does will endure forever; nothing can be added to it and nothing taken from it....

Ecclesiastes 3:14

The ninth inning ended in a tie ball game between Baylor University and the University of Texas, with the 1961 conference baseball championship still undecided between the two teams. Baylor needed to win the game to become conference champs; Texas could win the title with only a tie. Darkness had arrived and the umpire refused to let the game continue because Baylor's ballpark lacked lighting for night play. Because of the importance of the game, arrangements quickly took shape to transfer the game to a lighted ballpark across town. When Bibb Faulk, renowned coach of the Longhorns, received word of the plan he politely refused. How could he refuse? In the ensuing discussion around home plate among coaches and umpires, Coach Faulk referred to his well-used rule book and cited several rules releasing his team from any obligation to continue the game on another site or day. Thus, the game ended in a tie, and the Longhorns of Texas claimed the championship. Bibb Faulk had studied the rule book!

In similar fashion, Christian students need to study and internalize the Bible in order to compete effectively in college. Some might refer to the Bible as 'the Christian's rule book," but this title really minimizes the Bible's content because the Bible offers so much more. Yes, Biblical rules exist, mainly for our protection and for enabling relationship with God; but the Bible also reveals the nature of God, the grace of God, the expectations of God, and the wisdom of God, all spoken through God's chosen writers.

Let God's Word accompany you through daily study. Trying to obtain wisdom and knowledge in college without drawing from God's wisdom makes about as much sense as playing baseball in the dark. At times, the academic process will place the class spotlight on you; stand your ground with the Scriptures as your personal source of confidence. King Solomon captured the heart of the issue with these words: "I know that everything God does will endure forever...." This includes God's written Word!

WHAT'S THE IDEA?

The Lord brought me [wisdom] forth as the first of his works, before his deeds of old; I was appointed from eternity, from the beginning, before the world began....

Proverbs 8:22-23

Galileo Galilei (1564-1642), the great Italian astronomer, physicist, and mathematician ran into trouble with the Roman Catholic Church. Galileo (the name we recognize), through studying the heavens with his homemade telescope, came to agree with Copernicus (a Polish scientist) that the earth and other planets in our solar system revolve around the sun, a life-threatening conclusion for Galileo to reach. Unfortunately for Galileo, Catholic theologians had demanded scientists teach that the sun and planets revolve around the earth, based upon their interpretations of Scripture (notably Psalm 93:1, 96:10, 104:5; 1 Chronicles 16:30; Ecclesiastes 1:5). Today we chuckle at this obvious scientific and theological error, but for Galileo serious consequences accompanied his scientific discovery. Convicted as a heretic during the Inquisition and forced in the name of leniency to withdraw his support for a sun-centered system, Galileo received "only" the confinement of house arrest until his death about nine years later.

Our purpose rests beyond criticism of churches, religion, or science (yes, science can point to its own collection of foolish ideas in the past, too!); rather, our purpose is to point out the necessity of open and fair inquiry in the search for truth in any area of study. Sound familiar? It should, because as we stated in a previous devotional thought ("EYE-OPENER"), this comprises the goal of all academic process.

Do not fear ideas; evaluate them. "Evaluation" does not mean acceptance of every idea crossing your academic path, but it does mean considering ideas honestly in the light of current evidence and understanding. Further, particularly on social and theological issues, the Christian student needs to view complex problems through the "telescope" of God's Word. Look again at our Scripture reading for today. God's wisdom came before all else of His creation and will prevail through eternity. Best of all, God promises this wisdom to you. No fear!

TOUGH ISSUES

I [wisdom] was there when he set the heaven's in place, when he marked out the horizon on the face of the deep....

Proverbs 8:27

John Wayne dominated action movies for many years. Whether in cowboy, military, or other roles, audiences packed theaters to watch his hard-driving, two-fisted style in defeating evil; even today his movies appear on television with startling frequency. This popular actor developed a deep friendship with another equally tough individual named Ward Bond, who appeared in many of Wayne's films. Reportedly, these two close friends sometimes would feel a need to fight, thus, for fun they would take turns slugging each other in order to determine who best could absorb the other's punches. Such friendship! (Thankfully, I possess no friends who demand this type of fun, but I digress.)

Sometimes science and religion seem to express a similar need to punch one another. While progressing through your list of required college courses, inevitably the academic path will lead across past or present serious disagreements between science and religion. Some scholars point to Charles Darwin (1809-1882), a would-be theologian turned biologist, as instigator of the conflict, but a careful study of the history of science and religion takes the conflict much further back in time. Martin Luther (1483-1546), inspirational leader of the Protestant Revolution, and other historic notables had grappled with the conflict well before Darwin. Sadly, the conflict appears unlikely to end anytime soon.

Let's not minimize the seriousness of the conflict, but let's do formulate a proper prospective. Although sounding abstract and philosophical, recognize that issues of science and religion possess real consequences. For example, disagreements surrounding stem cell research have precipitated controversy and major political fallout in our country. As you approach issues of science and religion in the context of academic process, always remember the Scriptures and the enduring character of God. God created both science and religion, and ultimately they cannot contradict one another. Pray, then, for an ability to find and effectively present the truth.

GO ON OFFENSE

...for He guards the course of the just and protects the way of His faithful ones.

Proverbs 2:8

As the storm clouds of war approached France in the 1930's, French military planners convinced the government to construct a line of defensive, concrete fortifications and military facilities along their border with Germany, stretching from Switzerland to Luxembourg. Named the "Maginot Line," this massive engineering accomplishment promised to make France impenetrable to a German invasion force, or so everyone believed. However, as war came the Germans marched their army around the Maginot Line through Belgium and entered France while German airplanes simply flew over these fixed defensive fortifications. France fell in one month! Although the French effort stopped the Germans in a few places, generally, the Maginot Line stands as one of the greatest failures in military history.

In war and sports, a strong defense may help achieve victory. However, as the French learned, defense without a matching offensive capability usually foretells defeat. Perhaps surprisingly, your participation in the academic process likely will require you to assume both offensive and defensive positions in class discussions. In "going on offense," quickly learn that only documented information, not personal opinion, normally matters in these discussions; further, at no time should the discussion become personal in the sense of attacking or criticizing those with whom you disagree. "Going on offense" only means to politely but firmly push the point or position you have chosen to support.

Learn well the art of academic debate, a skill helpful in many areas of life. Modern Christianity cries out for gifted believers who not only can defend their faith, but who can go on offense effectively with the Good News of Jesus to a hardened world. Are you nervous about speaking in a college classroom or in sharing the Good News? Ponder Solomon's words from our Scripture reading for a moment: God "protects the way of His faithful ones." And He will protect you. Go on offense!

KEEP COOL

A fool gives full vent to his anger, but a wise man keeps himself under control.

Proverbs 29:11

Pat Head Summitt, celebrated coach of the University of Tennessee Lady Vols basketball team, exemplified "coolness under fire." Whether in the course of winning one of her eight(!) national championships, claiming victory in more than 1000 games (making her the most successful coach in NCAA basketball history), or in losing a game or a championship, this coach maintained her public composure. (Coach Summit did foster a reputation for attention-getting motivational talks behind closed doors if her team played poorly.) Even in pregnancy, Coach Summit exemplified cool, calm control. While on a recruiting flight to another state, she went into labor; instead of landing and heading for the nearest hospital, the famed coach insisted the pilot return to Tennessee for the birth of her son. Cool and Calm!

Take a look at the really successful people in your world and compare them to the example above. Most successful people maintain their public composure no matter how difficult, or enjoyable, the circumstances. In numerous writings, including today's verse, King Solomon makes reference to this ability to control one's emotions. (See Proverbs 16:32, 19:11, and 25:28 for other examples.) In Proverbs 17:27 Solomon speaks of an "even-tempered" person by using a Hebrew word, *qar-ruah*, which literally means "cool spirit." Thus, many years ago Solomon recognized the need for self control in human relationships.

In the academic realm, you undoubtedly will encounter erroneous ideas and unpleasant people (both students and professors). Use the academic process as a training ground for developing self-control, a lifetime asset. Learn to transition erroneous ideas into truthful ones and to deal patiently with unpleasant associates--all in a gracious manner. In doing so, you will develop important leadership skills for the future. Remember Solomon's advice: "a wise man keeps himself under control." Keep cool!

GOOD GRACIOUSNESS

The wise in heart are called discerning, and pleasant words promote instruction.

Proverbs 16:21

Dr. Martin Luther King, Jr. possessed a vision for America, a vision so dramatic he gave his life for it. While not a perfect man, Dr. King eloquently voiced a perfect message to America centered upon fairness and equality for all citizens, non-violence, and a genuine love and respect for Jesus and his teachings. Often the focus of cruelty, Dr. King was spit upon, beaten, stabbed, jailed, bombed, and publicly criticized (sometimes even by other civil rights leaders). Yet through these many discouraging events until his death in 1968, Dr. King spoke his unwavering message of love and forgiveness to a hard-hearted nation. In the manner of heroes, he gave his life for a just cause, a cause that in the end shook and changed the foundations of America. As writer Philip Yancey[6] noted about the Nobel Peace Prize winner: "King had developed a sophisticated strategy of war fought with grace, not guns."* Take note of *grace.*

As a college student, most of the professors will stimulate your learning and reasoning abilities. Rarely will a professor criticize a student's faith and beliefs directly, nor usually will professors try to force acceptance of an idea or concept. However, a few zealous academics seem to forget the rules of academic process when speaking on topics of great concern and passion to themselves. In other words, sometimes only supportive or negative ideas may be presented and condescending statements may be made about those who hold differing views. Be careful with these professors, because they may become vindictive in their responses (and grades!). These professors violate the vital academic purposes of fairness and the open search for truth.

In dealing with professors who violate academic process, always go to class well-prepared and use the academic process to make your points while countering theirs. Above all, consider Dr. King's approach and act with grace toward others holding different viewpoints from your own. By doing so, even those who reach opposing conclusions will admire your character.

---

[6] Yancey, Philip. *Soul Survivor.* New York: Doubleday, 2001.

CHRISTIAN ADVANTAGE

For the Lord gives wisdom, and from his mouth come knowledge and understanding.

Proverbs 2:6

Let's state the obvious about basketball: greater height usually confers substantial advantage. In the National Basketball Association (NBA), former dominant players like Shaquille O'Neal (7'1"), Kevin Garnett (6'11"), and Yao Ming (7'6") make the point. The reasons stand out clearly; with a fixed goal height at ten feet, and with rebounding and blocking the opponent's shot such integral parts of the game, height matters. Even the traditionally shorter guard positions now frequently favor taller players. (At 6'9" tall, the former great player, Michael "Magic" Johnson, shattered the idea of "short only" at guard.) Although basketball requires great skill of every player, height usually confers competitive advantages.

Somewhat like the advantages conferred by height in basketball, Christians should enjoy advantages over others in the academic realm. Surprised? Students who spend minimal time studying Scripture sometimes express genuine perplexity at this "new" thought; but it's true. Not only addressed in numerous verses and chapters by King Solomon, other Biblical writers echo the same thought. James, in writing to Jewish Christians of his day, states: "If any of you lack wisdom, he should ask God, who gives generously to all without finding fault...." (James 1:5) The Bible offers a consistent message, a message promising greater wisdom (and understanding) to the faithful who ask.

As you learn and work through the academic process of college, make dependence upon God's wisdom through daily prayer and Bible study a central part of your life. Increased wisdom and enhanced learning ability come as by-products of sincere commitment and faith. In other words, God requires humility and close relationship with Him before the transfer of wisdom can occur; non-believers need not apply for this intellectual "power boost." Reach beyond yourself by claiming God's promises. As a result of faith, you will gain the "Christian advantage."

Unit Six

Money Magic

Managing money while in college requires discipline, determination, and foresight. Unlike some of the more philosophical units preceding this one, financial issues comprise a very real, day-to-day worry for many students. Not only must students worry about the academic side of college, but as costs soar, paying for college introduces an increasingly difficult set of problems. Thus, many students must become very nimble in juggling academic responsibilities with work schedules in order to stay in school. For many students, skill at financial planning may make the difference between success and failure.

What do we mean by "financial planning"? Financial planning means constructing and living within a budget for both college costs and daily living expenses. It means knowing how to find sources of funding for college fees. It means learning to minimize debt. Actually, financial planning means many things related to responsible money management. In this unit, we want to explore a number of the dimensions surrounding wise use of your money.

In my experience as a professor, the number one hindrance to successful completion of college for a large number of students relates to money. Surprisingly, many Christian students fail to engage in formal planning about finances, often seeming to take the path of least resistance without fully considering where the path may lead. It is as if some magic ending will arrive to make everything okay.

Finally, some students find financial planning a boring topic. However, consider this: the Bible tells us that money (and other resources) come from God's hand, and therefore, God expects us to plan and manage wisely. Learning financial planning in college will provide skills useful after college at home and professionally. In other words, in learning to plan financially, we develop a set of skills necessary for successful living. Bring a positive attitude as we now consider your college finances.

HAW, HAW!

Whoever trusts in his riches will fall, but the righteous will thrive like a green leaf.

Proverbs 11:28

Fabulously wealthy, Horace Austin Warner "Haw" Tabor became a legend in Colorado. Worth approximately $100 million in the 1880's (billions of dollars in today's money), "Silver Dollar" Tabor possessed it all, including silver mines, land, businesses, and prestige. A friend of politicians, business tycoons, and American Presidents, Tabor and his beautiful wife, Baby Doe, lived a spontaneous life of luxury and extravagance, at least until the money ran out. Imagine trying to negotiate a business deal, as Tabor did, only to find no money in your "empire," and further, debts of over a million dollars carried your signature. Haw Tabor died in 1899 a poor man; Baby Doe died thirty-seven years later, a deranged, pitiful, lonely woman. The Tabors learned the hard way about the importance of developing a financial plan and sticking to it.

Actually, history offers many examples of people like Haw Tabor who made and lost vast sums because they failed to distinguish between *making* and *keeping* a fortune. Everyone--from wealthiest to least wealthy--ought to formulate and live by a personalized financial plan. To do otherwise invites unpleasant surprises and perhaps financial disaster. College students are no exception!

Once the task of developing a financial plan reaches completion, you then possess a diagram of the future not previously held. Even though the plan may require some adjustments along the way as unforeseen income and expense surprises occur, the end result will provide a much better grasp of your financial situation while proceeding through college.

In the next devotion, we will discuss the basics of creating an actual financial plan. For now, however, pledge to yourself and God to manage your money responsibly. Then ask for God's leadership in developing a plan. After all, the money belongs to Him.

BLUEPRINTS AND PLANS

Discretion will protect you, and understanding will guard you.
Proverbs 2:11

A good financial plan serves your financial needs in much the same way a blueprint provides directions for constructing a building. In the previous devotional thought, we demonstrated the need for sound financial planning. Now let's consider some of the necessary features of the plan. Remember, a financial plan provides a broad, but detailed, look at your finances over an extended period of time.

Begin the process by setting financial goals for your college years. May I suggest two for consideration: 1. To spend money wisely; 2. To graduate from college with no debt (more about this later). These goals, or others of your choosing, will give direction to the main part of the financial plan, namely, creating a budget.

In concept, creating a budget employs the simple concept of balancing expected income with projected expenditures. Doing this involves listing all probable income and expenses and calculating how much can be spent on each item on a monthly, weekly, or daily basis. Although requiring time to construct, a well-considered expenditure list becomes invaluable for clarifying the expense side of the budget.

Within your budget under "expenses," make a distinction between fixed costs (tuition, fees, books, and rent usually change little from one semester to another) and discretionary costs (food, gasoline, extracurricular activities, and going out with friends can vary considerably, depending upon your preferences and habits). Controlling discretionary spending frequently presents severe challenges for new college students. Once you have allocated various amounts of money for all of the categories and items, keeping up with expenditures on a daily and weekly basis becomes critical to success in living within the budget. Available commercial software, although not required, offers help in the entire budgeting process.

Other aspects of financial planning will receive attention in devotional pages to come. For now, exercise "discretion" and "understanding" as your beginning points.

OF GOLDEN RULES

...the borrower is servant to the lender.

Proverbs 22:7b

King Solomon got it painfully right! Borrow money and become "servant to the lender." Sometimes the truth hurts, but many college students upon reaching graduation find themselves entrapped by overwhelming debt that suddenly looks impossible to escape--often for many years. Graduates generally find small consolation in knowing their debt accumulated for the noble purpose of education. Debt is debt and must be repaid (plus interest)!

Learn the Golden Rule of financial planning early in life by applying it to your college experience. Briefly stated, the Golden Rule requires two words: avoid debt. Easing into serious debt often comes incrementally and quietly; thus, several subsequent devotions will discuss issues of debt avoidance. For now, however, begin thinking about the "slippery slopes" of life that potentially may slide a well-meaning person (that's you) into debt. Then, visualize debt as your enemy!

Several good reasons exist for viewing debt as the enemy. For example, working to pay down debt (the result of a past decision) usually deprives the debtor of money to invest in the future. In extreme (but all too common) cases, particularly when students borrow for both undergraduate and graduate school, the debt may destroy a person's financial future for life, erasing even the ability to invest for retirement. What's more, if marriage and family enter the picture, paying for family expenses may prove difficult because of the old debts from college days. Too, constantly worrying about debt frequently robs the joy from everyday living. Repeat after me: "avoid debt."

I believe a determined student can uncover ways of avoiding nearly all college debt, with God's help. Why do I believe this? Because I have seen many self-supporting students accomplish this feat. Yes, it takes faith and effort, but that characterizes the Christian's life anyway. Pray for God's guidance in avoiding the quicksand of debt.

FIND A WAY

Hope deferred makes the heart sick, but a longing fulfilled is a tree of life.
Proverbs 13:12

According to the latest *Post-Secondary Student Aid Survey*, published by the U.S. Department of Education, two-thirds of all college seniors carry outstanding loan balances, with average debt hovering around $25,000. This figure tends to obscure the very large debts on the upper end of the scale (ten percent of college graduates owe over $35,000 at completion, and graduates from professional schools typically may owe $150,000 or more). Throw in interest charges with these loans and the debts reach dizzying proportions for a young person.

With rapidly rising college costs, how may students hope to avoid accumulated debt? Since the long answer requires many pages, let's look at some quick suggestions for you to research. First, be prepared to work for wages, even if it lengthens your stay in college; many businesses offer work opportunities for students. Second, shop for the best deal in a college. For example, a community college may offer real cost advantages along with excellent teaching faculty for your first two years. Further, and perhaps a surprise, private schools often provide great scholarship opportunities. Contact financial aid departments for further information about scholarships, work-study programs, and grants at colleges of interest.

Consider, too, the military. Every military branch provides opportunities for covering the costs of college; thus you will need to shop around. Some of the best programs originate close to home through the National Guard. Although varying by state, in Pennsylvania, for example, the Guard will pay all (tuition) expenses to any state college or university and even may send you to graduate or professional school! Your on-going obligation includes one weekend a month and two weeks training per year, with a salary paid for your time on the job. Further, additional paid duty assignments often are available during the summer for students. Check it out in your state.

Listen to Solomon. Fulfill the longing for a college education, but do not let lingering debt make you heart-sick. With God's wisdom, you can find a way to avoid college debt.

K(NO)W CREDIT CARDS

He who rebukes a man will in the end gain more favor than he who has a flattering tongue.

Proverbs 28:23

King Solomon apparently cared little for "political correctness." Time and again he spoke bluntly and forcefully to his readers. "Fools," especially, grated on Solomon's emotions, and consequently, he directed numerous literary jabs at this particular group (take a look at Proverbs 26:3 for a sample). In keeping with our Bible verse for today, I need to follow Solomon's lead in scolding a sizable number of students. However, rather than "fools" I believe "foolish" is the better word to use here.

Think ten years beyond college graduation, when each month you pay down debt on clothes and pizza purchased with credit-cards as an undergraduate. Preposterous? Not really. This scenario takes place much more frequently than you might believe. Compared to college loans, credit-card debt stems from different sources, and the rules and interest charges vary considerably; but in the end, credit-card debt amounts to a *high interest rate loan*. Further, not only do interest rates typically reach the stratosphere, but other unpleasant features include finance charges, annual fees, cash advance fees, and late payment fees (which may raise interest rates even higher). If these facts do not deter you, then consider numerous recent studies indicating that careless buying habits often accompany credit-card use, meaning "plastic" users usually purchase more things at higher prices than cash purchasers. Thus, how you pay seems to influence how much you pay!

As a college freshman, you likely will receive numerous invitations, in person or by mail, to apply for credit-cards. The sales pitch usually contains the elements of status and easy money; and for the final touch a low "teaser rate" makes the offer seem like a great opportunity. (The low teaser rate soon will morph into a very high rate.) Credit-card issuers want you in debt so they can profit; treat credit card "invitations" like you would treat poison ivy. Do not act foolishly. Know credit-cards: no credit-cards.

TRUTH AND CONSEQUENCES

A good name is more desirable than great riches; to be esteemed is better than silver of gold.

Proverbs 22:1

Look into the future at your first job after college. Let's say your salary approximates the national average for recent college graduates of about $35,000 per year; and since unfortunately you failed to heed the advice about avoiding long-term debt in college, you owe about $20,000 on the popular Stafford Loan program. You likewise owe some credit-card debt. Using the standard 6.8% interest rate required on Stafford Loans, your monthly payments for ten years will come to over $200, this on top of regular living expenses, taxes, and various deductions from your monthly paycheck. Finally, stuck on a tread mill of work and debt, you decide to find an escape from all debts and start over financially. Thus, the question: Do good alternatives exist for escaping loan debts?

Truthfully no, and the consequences of walking away from your loan debts promise grim results. Let's look at several common tactics and outcomes. First, "loan forbearance" sometimes provides a brief reprieve from payments, but in the end this tactic piles interest charges even higher and increases the debt load. Second, and worse still, are the effects of defaulting on loans. Your credit rating will suffer greatly, and the government can intercept tax refunds, garnish wages, and withhold Social Security and other federal benefits. Third, filing for bankruptcy seldom works with student loans today, because of tightened bankruptcy reform laws enacted in recent years.

Our discussion so far covers strictly monetary and legal considerations. But, for Christians we need to inquire about God's thoughts on the matter. In other words, what does God think of his followers trying to run from legitimate debts? Seeking an easy way out from debt when others acted in good faith by lending you money violates numerous commands and ethical standards in Scripture (for example, see Luke 16:10-11). Honor your financial obligations as a tribute to God and watch your "good name" grow.

JUST SAY "NO"

He who puts up security for another will surely suffer, but whoever refuses to strike hands in pledge is safe.

Proverbs 11:15

Talk about scary! Think about the tremendous dollar losses in financial markets of the United States during the subprime mortgage industry "meltdown" of 2007-2008. For example, the Federal National Mortgage Association and the Federal Home Loan and Mortgage Corporation, two government-sponsored enterprises, took particularly large losses because home buyers became unable to pay for mortgages owned by these two giant organizations. Fannie Mae and Freddie Mac, as these institutions are known respectively, faced disaster with debts of over 1.5 trillion dollars between them. Fortunately for them, the American taxpayer stepped forward and helped bail them out of the dilemma.

In pondering the entire episode, one wonders how such well-educated people with nearly infinite resources could have exercised such poor professional judgment and skill. It boggles the mind. Thus, Freddie Mac and Fannie Mae ought to teach everyone a valuable lesson about lending money to uncertain sources. As a college student, at some point one (or more) of your friends may ask to borrow money from you. Be careful, and ask yourself several questions: "If the person lacks money now, what gives me confidence of their ability to pay the money back later?" "Do I really have money to lend (and maybe lose)?" "Will misunderstanding over this "loan" potentially cause hard feelings and damage a friendship?" "Do I know for certain the intended use of the borrowed money?"

King Solomon delivered an emphatic statement about the risks of lending money to others (see also Proverbs 6:1-5). When asked for money by friends or acquaintances, be pleasant but firm. Plainly tell them that you operate on a strict budget, and because this, you cannot lend money. If Fannie Mae and Freddie Mac can make poor loans, so can you. Just say "no"!

GOD'S RENT

Honor the Lord with your wealth, with the firstfruits of all your crops....
Proverbs 3:9

I recently heard a respected pastor quip: "Tithing is paying the rent on God's stuff." Admittedly this pastor possesses a well-developed sense of humor, but the more I thought about the statement, the more in agreement I found myself. I imagine this witticism fails to capture the full spirit of tithing presented in Scripture, but it cleverly reminds us of several truths, particularly regarding our financial responsibilities to God.

In examining the concept of tithing, several important components emerge. For example, God's ownership of all material things, including land, food, and money, creates the basis for our returning at least 10% to Him (see Leviticus 27:30). On this note, some people argue that giving their time in tithe is a legitimate substitute for giving their money. Surely, God expects us to use our time for Him as indicated in both Old and New Testaments; but tithing as defined in Scripture requires giving of material resources.

Actually, the New Testament suggests our giving without strict percentages as the Holy Spirit and our love for God direct us; in other words, we often may need to give more than 10%. Mosaic Law, repeated in today's verse by King Solomon, required giving the best of the first produce ("firstfruits") of the harvest to honor God (see Exodus 23:19). As New Testament Christians, we must tithe from the front end of our paycheck, not from the leftovers. Why? Because God tells us to tithe this way. Further, and of great importance, returning the "firstfruits" displays our faith in God's ability to provide for us.

College students sometimes insist on not tithing because of limited finances. To the contrary, this presents exactly the reason for tithing--giving as a sign of our faith in God. Solomon flatly states another Biblical truth in Proverbs 3:10: God will bless you in some way for your faithfulness in giving. As a cornerstone of sound financial planning, resolve to tithe while in college even if your tithe seems to resemble the "widow's mite" (Mark 12:41-44). Pay the "rent"!

BUSINESS 101

Dishonest money dwindles away, but he who gathers money little by little makes it grow.
Proverbs 13:11

Picture a lovely rustic home tucked within 100 acres of woodland, canoeing on mountain streams, daily hikes viewing wildlife and wildflowers, bicycle riding on country lanes, and freedom from financial worries. Sound good? Such is the life of one of my best friends and his energetic wife. However, to assume all this came easily for them overlooks the truth. Their success came as the result of setting financial and life goals, living a modest lifestyle, and striving with unwavering determination to meet their goals until retirement. When people ask my friend how to become wealthy he smiles and says, "I don't know how to get rich quickly, but I am pretty certain I know how to build wealth slowly." Wise words, but King Solomon said them first!

Through the years as I have listened to a cross-section of local society ask me for advice about financial planning and investing, the recurring message has been one of uncertainty and frustration. Medical doctors, nurses, educators, pastors, students and many others often speak of their lack of training and understanding in the world of business and their lack of confidence regarding investing. This should not surprise anyone because most college students, unless they major in business or economics, simply miss any basic financial training in college.

The business of life requires attention (but not obsession). For you and your family, considerations such as insurance, healthcare, budgeting, investing, retirement planning, and other issues become necessary elements of living, regardless of profession. As a college student, consider using some of your elective hours to take a general business class and a beginning economics sequence as preparation for the business realities of life.

For an encouraging footnote to the story of my friends described in the first paragraph, let's tell the rest of their story. When married after college, their joined worldly possessions consisted mostly of an old Volvo and a canoe. But with goals and a plan they became wealthy. Oh, and did I mention their professions? Both were teachers!

PERCEPTIONS

Do not wear yourself out to get rich; have the wisdom to show restraint.
Proverbs 23:4

As a geology teacher, traveling in the western United States provides great satisfaction and intrigue for me. Many parts of the Rocky Mountains and adjacent lands consist of geologic features and formations rich in clues regarding the geologic history of these regions. Through the years, frequent family vacations to these regions provided me with volumes of photographs and new perspectives to share with my college classes. Yet for all of my trips in the West, the one simple experience I can never fully explain or adjust to involves perception of distance. Distant objects like mountain ranges seem deceptively close when, in reality, many miles may separate them from me. In short, sometimes my perception leads to poor conclusions.

In life, as in geology, our perceptions sometimes may lead us to draw damaging, or at least unwise, conclusions of great consequence to our joy and purpose in life. Nowhere do I see this more than in the context of students making career choices based on aspirations of wealth, as though wealth were a magic tonic for life's problems. Rather than review the many aspects of selecting a major and career discussed in an earlier unit, let's just say that wealth should become a by-product of career choice, not the goal. God expects you to become a good manager of the money and resources entrusted to you, but more importantly He wants allegiance to His will, not to making money.

King Solomon told us plainly: "Do not wear yourself out to get rich...." Keep life's important things in focus, like family, friends, joy in living each day, and studying for a career that excites you. Always--always--pray and listen to God's response, and then act accordingly. Your perceptions and reality will fit together much more closely.

Unit Seven

To Your Good Health

Throughout my years of teaching and working with college students, "healthful living" rarely, if ever, came up for discussion. Many students fail to anticipate the sizable physical and mental demands of college life and seemingly give little attention or preparation to this very important topic. Think for a moment about the many ways good health, or poor health, impacts the way you feel, think, and act. Then imagine the typical high-stress environment associated with college academic and social life (not to mention job demands if employed), and a picture begins to emerge about the need for healthful living if you wish to achieve success as a student.

In this unit, developing healthful habits will be viewed in a broad sense, pertaining not only to physical concerns but also to the mental, emotional, and spiritual dimensions of health. This broad view of human health actually defines the focal point of modern medicine today. Thus, we often hear of "holistic healing" in the medical sciences, a concept defining treatment of the total person in contrast to treating only physical symptoms.

As we discuss multiple aspects of health as portrayed by the Bible, remember your status in life as a college student. Adulthood arrives quickly and with it the responsibility of caring for yourself in many areas of life. Even if you commute to classes each day as a stay-at-home student, the job of self-maintenance should shift to your shoulders and out of the hands of others, notably parents. Finally, the principles of healthful living learned as a college student should apply throughout life. Learn your health lessons well and stick to them!

A MATTER OF BALANCE

Do not be wise in your own eyes; fear the Lord and shun evil. This will bring health to your body and nourishment to your bones.

Proverbs 3:7-8

Asian snow leopards inhabit some of the most remote and formidable environments on earth. Images of exotic snow-capped mountain ranges such as the Himalayas, Hindu Kush, Pamirs, and the Tian Shan necessarily enter any discussion of these amazing felines. Like all of the world's big cats, their numbers continue to diminish at an alarming rate, largely because of human activities. Fortunately, scientists today are learning more about these creatures in an effort to save them from extinction.

Oddly, snow leopards possess very long tails. Normally the tails extend about the same length as the animal's body, or about four feet. Scientists now know of various important functions for this tail. For example, the cat may wrap the tail around itself during bitterly cold temperatures for warmth, or it may sometimes use the tail to entice its prey. But most importantly, in treacherous mountains with thousand-foot drops at nearly every turn, the long tails keep these cats from falling in the rocky terrain. In other words, these unusual tails provide balance.

In a figurative sense, college students--like the snow leopards--need balance in their lives for healthful living and academic success. Research by modern medical science provides confirmation of the advice given by mothers to their children since the beginning of time: eat a balanced diet, rest sufficiently, and exercise regularly. King Solomon added a fourth part to healthful living as seen in our Scripture reference, that is to worship and serve God. Sadly, with the rigors of college life, many students frequently fail to achieve a proper balance among these requirements for good health and learning efficiency.

Discipline yourself to live a healthy lifestyle. Eat, rest, and exercise properly, and support this with a dedication to grow spiritually through your four years in college. You will be happier, healthier, and your grades will show it. It's all a matter of balance.

LET'S EAT!

If you find honey, eat just enough--too much of it, and you will vomit.
Proverbs 25:16

One of my friends and I drove to the Great Smoky Mountains for a day of hiking. In the little foothills community of Townsend, Tennessee, my friend pulled into a service station and filled his car with fuel; a mile or so later we parked and began our day of hiking. Upon returning later in the day, the car would not start. After considerable frustration and an expensive towing bill, a mechanic finally diagnosed the problem. Instead of filling the fuel tank with gasoline, my friend mistakenly had filled the tank with diesel fuel--a very bad thing to do to a gasoline engine. Why? Gasoline engines, by design, simply will not run properly on the wrong fuel.

In many respects, the human body reminds us of a machine. Although decidedly more adaptable than a car engine, fed improper fuel (food) the human body ceases to function efficiently. Today, modern science knows a great deal about the energy and nutrient requirements of the human body and the foods necessary for healthful living. For example, the brain requires energy for proper functioning, and that means plenty of glucose from fresh fruits and vegetables. Also, the brain needs abundant protein in order for neurotransmitters to send proper electrical messages around the body. And so it goes throughout the body. Specific organs demand specific nutrient and energy levels. Bottom line? Individuals need a balanced diet consumed three times per day, using moderation in portion sizes.

Now consider a typical college student's diet. Preferred foods such as pizza, burgers, fries, soft drinks, junk food from the vending machines, and cookies from home, consumed at all hours of the day or night and often in large quantities, hardly qualify as a balanced, healthful, brain-stimulating diet. The results of such diets are numerous, often including weight gain and diminished academic prowess. Many years ago, King Solomon urged dietary discipline. Take his advice and learn about the foods you consume. Your body will say "thanks."

WEIGHT A MINUTE

All man's efforts are for his mouth, yet his appetite is never satisfied.
Ecclesiastes 6:7

Weight-gain in college provides steady fodder for campus humorists. Further, the "freshman fifteen" often stands as an expectation rather than a warning to beginning college students. But would you like to know a secret? Gaining excessive weight in college is neither funny nor unavoidable. To the contrary, weight-gain casts a sad commentary on an increasingly obese, unhealthy society, at least according to many health and medical officials.

In its *Dietary Guidelines for Americans 2005,* the U.S. Department of Agriculture (USDA) cites research indicating a doubling of obesity in the United States in the last twenty years. More specifically, obesity in young people has skyrocketed. In a sobering touch, the USDA lists at least twelve serious health risks arising from obesity. Thus, based upon available research, the USDA presents clear conclusions: Americans (including college students) need to consume fewer calories, exercise regularly, and make wiser food choices. Pretty simple!

On the other hand, this is college where nearly everything--meetings, study times, social interaction--revolves around munching on something, something usually high in calories and fat. Temptations abound, and everyone, it seems, takes part. Further, the self-delusions that "I've never had a weight problem...." or "I can lose a few pounds if I need to...." apparently become excuses for careless eating. Remember, however, modern studies demonstrate conclusively that losing weight and keeping it off require much more effort than putting it on.

Let's be reasonable. No one is suggesting that you never eat a slice of pizza or make a late night run to the Waffle House; becoming a social iceberg creates little joy. On the other hand, you do need to exercise restraint and discipline by largely shunning harmful foods loaded with sugar and fat in favor of a balanced diet. Try not to confirm King Solomon's cynical statement found in today's Scripture reference. Rather, practice the old adage: "Eat to live; do not live to eat!"

EXERCISE PRUDENCE

You who are simple gain prudence; you who are foolish, gain understanding.
Proverbs 8:5

When I think back to my boyhood days (far too many years ago!), I remember admonitions from my parents and school teachers about the need for exercise; my chubbiness seemed to attract advice I did not seek. In those days, "exercise" usually meant jumping jacks, push-ups, sit-ups, and various other weird movements created mostly for playing sports and less for building healthy bodies. I fondly remember my father deciding that exercise would help my athletic career--I was about ten years of age. Each morning at 6 a.m. Dad would "assist" me out of bed, dress me in a drab, gray sweat-suit, and lead me through the chosen exercises. In my early morning sleep stupor the exercise routine apparently failed to achieve the desired results, because Dad ceased the program after several weeks.

Now fast forward to the present. Today, "exercise" can mean dozens of interesting pursuits, each with its own fashion mode and each possessing a cult-like following. Hiking, rock climbing, kayaking, and dancing all make the list of fun exercise pursuits. Drive along nearly any roadway in America and watch the walkers, joggers, and runners. Boy, things have changed from sit-ups, push-ups, and gray sweat-suits! Actually, this change represents great progress, for many people enjoy physical activity and understand the health benefits of exercise.

Even so, I mix with many likable folks who refuse to exercise, usually because they "lack the time." Such foolishness! Based upon mounds of research, medical science points to numerous and significant health benefits from exercise, including combating chronic diseases, assisting in weight management, strengthening heart and lungs, and adjusting our moods, to name a few. Benefits accrue for efforts of only twenty minutes to an hour each day (depending upon the exercise). Consider King Solomon's perspective on living. In order to become a better student and to enjoy better health, wise-up and get with an exercise program!

SLEEP SPEAK

The sleep of a laborer is sweet, whether he eats little or much, but the abundance of a rich man permits him no sleep.

Proverbs 5:12

How much sleep do you need each night? Probably more than you might imagine. I regularly hear college students declare their ability to "get by" on four or five hours per night. A little self-deception apparently stretches a long way, because modern medicine tells a very different story about our need for rest. Most sleep authorities recommend about nine hours of sleep each night for teenagers and seven to eight hours for adults.

Biologically sleep constitutes a necessity for humans, not a luxury. With regularly inadequate amounts of sleep, negative results occur. Daytime drowsiness, inability to concentrate, irritability, lower productivity, and decreased motor skills frequently develop. As just one example, driver fatigue, according to the National Highway Safety Administration, causes over 100,000 vehicle accidents and 1,500 deaths per year in the United States. On the positive side, adequate sleep helps our immune system fight diseases (like the common cold), gives down time for resupplying energy to brain cells and for repairing of neurons in our nervous system, and enables hormone releases instrumental in regulating body functions. Face it, you need sleep!

Sleeping adequately amid the stress and activity of college life requires willful choice. Anyone who has lived in a college dorm or apartment remembers the constant flow of temptations to socialize and participate in activities often more appealing than studying. In my assessment, the most commonly wasted time slot occurs in the early evening after dinner. Thus, an hour or two of unproductive time here with the resulting delay in study activity often means late hours and missed sleep. Consider this helpful tip: condition yourself to begin studying within a few minutes of completing the evening meal.

In the verse quoted above, King Solomon recognized stress as another factor in the sleep equation, an observation confirmed by modern research. Develop discipline in your study habits, supported with prayer for God's help in academic achievement. This sequence will result in better grades, lowered stress, and nights of great sleep.

SNAKE BITES

In the end it [alcohol] bites like a snake and poisons like a viper.
Proverbs 23:32

One of the great contradictions in American life pertains to colleges and universities. On the one hand, collectively the brightest and most capable young people attend college. But on the other hand, many of these same intelligent students may participate willingly in some of the world's most destructive behavior involving alcohol and drug use. Looked at from nearly any perspective, most institutions of higher learning inadvertently have become centers for substance abuse, and the results are shocking.

Alcohol, of course, ranks as the number one abused drug on most college campuses, apparently viewed by many as a rite of passage into the adult world. Anyone familiar with behavioral rites in higher education realizes the enormous social pressure on students at many college campuses to drink frequently and excessively. Colleges consequently produce lots of alcoholics and alcohol-related problems. Although impossible to condense all of the vast array of problems into a simple statement here, let me mention just a few statistics[7] to make a point about the nasty annual effects of alcohol on college life: about 600,000 college students experience injury, and 1,700 die; 700;000 students assault others; almost 100,000 students experience sexual assault or date rape; over 2 million students drive drunk; 400,000 engage in unsafe sex; and 25% of all college students report academic problems as a result of their drinking habits. No, you will not see any of these statistics on television beer commercials, but the truth remains. You might think about potential consequences when a beer ad talks of the "good life."

King Solomon spoke pointedly about the life-destroying effects of alcohol abuse; his description of intoxication contained in Proverbs 23:29-35 sounds like a modern observation. Just why some people become alcoholics is a complicated medical issue involving genetics, age, family history, emotional make-up, and others. However, regardless of causes I doubt if anyone ever intends to become an alcoholic, yet, it happens. Abstinence wears well for a Christian; beware of snakes that bite!

---

[7] NIAAA (National Institute on Alcohol Abuse and Alcoholism), 7/11/2007, USA.gov.

HYGIENE HIGHLIGHTS

He who obeys instructions guards his life, but he who is contemptuous of his ways will die.

Proverbs 19:16

Underlying this unit about healthful living stands a principle: good health boosts academic achievement. Thus, preventing illness should become an important enterprise for all college students. Because of the nearness of students to one another in dormitories, cafeterias, classrooms, and social events, the prospect of shared diseases looms large unless students exercise caution and sound hygiene. Sadly, research shows many individuals failing to take basic precautions necessary for staying well.

Leaf through nearly any introductory biology or health book and find chapters regarding germs. Various properties of different germs stagger the imagination, particularly the ability of microorganisms to survive and multiply. For example, bacteria may double in population every twenty minutes; five bacteria on a sandwich at noon would multiply to ten million by 7:00 p.m. Further, bacteria may survive up to two hours on dry surfaces such as door handles and computer keyboards. If these figures do not impress, think of 21,000 germs per square inch on a typical work desk (that's 400 times more than the typical toilet seat!) or 229,000 germs per square inch on frequently used faucet handles (are you grossed-out yet?). As you might guess, numerous diseases from common colds to hepatitis A and salmonellosis can be passed along when we touch contaminated surfaces with our hands and then put our unwashed hands to our mouth, nose, or eyes. If everyone simply scrubbed their hands regularly, especially after coughing, sneezing, and using the toilet, the incidence of illness nationwide would drop significantly.

In addition to the thoughts discussed above, be aware that college presents many opportunities for friends to pass contagious diseases to friends in the most innocent and unintended ways. Sharing towels, clothes, eating utensils, drinks, and romance present risks. For your own health and safety, obey the instructions of medical science and practice sound hygiene. Here's to your good health!

LIFE PRESERVER

Wisdom is a shelter as money is a shelter, but the advantage of knowledge is this: that wisdom preserves the life of its possessor.
Ecclesiastes 7:12

HIV/AIDS claims the title as the world's most devastating epidemic in recent years. Beginning with the first general recognition of the deadly disease in the early 1980's, medical geographers report that in roughly twenty years the infection numbers climbed from a few hundred thousand in Africa to over forty million worldwide, with millions dead as the result. Africa, as the epicenter of the catastrophe, remains a tragedy; but, India, China, Russia, and several Caribbean countries also stand squarely in the path of this developing storm with no end in sight.

Okay, HIV/AIDS is admittedly a stunning world dilemma, but do I need to worry about it in the United States? Isn't the disease pretty much under control here? And, besides, isn't the disease restricted mostly to homosexuals? Think again! This disease continues to spread in America throughout all segments of the population. Recently, the U.S. Centers for Prevention and Disease Control presented figures showing the annual average of new HIV infections in recent years at about 55,000 cases. To make matters worse for the unsuspecting, infected persons may carry the virus for a decade or more without knowing it or showing visible signs of the disease. However, these same persons can transmit the virus to others, often through sexual intercourse. Beware!

Given Hollywood's (and other media's) great hypocrisy in glamorizing promiscuous sexual behavior in the face of the current AIDS epidemic, one can imagine many college students ignoring the threat and living very dangerously. On the other hand, when numerous other debilitating, sexually-transmitted diseases take their place in the list of possibilities along with AIDS, the glamour of promiscuity should diminish in favor of fear.

Take King Solomon's advice and make wisdom your guide. Shield your life through good judgment and discipline, even when others do not. By living as Christ would have us to live, you will avoid the physical and emotional risks of promiscuous sexual behavior, thereby preserving your life and the lives of others. But you already knew this, didn't you?

NO MOM

Listen, my son, to your father's instruction and do not forsake your mother's teaching.

Proverbs 1:8

King Solomon noted a difference in approach between many mothers and fathers interacting with their children. Did you catch this difference in our Scripture verse? Notice the two words "instruction" and "teaching" with similar, but not the same, meanings. Instruction, from the father, suggests an air of control, perhaps even command; whereas, teaching, by the mother, presents a gentler picture of interaction and demonstration to the child. Can you relate to King Solomon's observation? I think many of us do.

For the majority of us, I suspect, the valuable lessons we learned about managing illnesses and first aid emergencies came from the "teaching" of our mothers. These memories and lessons we cherish. But, guess what...mom will not be with you in college, and it will be your responsibility to handle illnesses and first aid emergencies. Plan on them because they will happen.

For medical events too small to involve the college's infirmary or a local hospital, you should maintain a medical kit with easy access in your dormitory room or apartment. Maintaining the "medicine box" became standard procedure for our three children (with mom's help) during their college years. You might consider including the following items in your kit: band-aids and antibiotic cream or ointment for cuts, an anti-itch cream for insect bites, ibuprofen or equivalent for headaches and fever, over-the-counter remedies for nausea and diarrhea, a decongestant, and a non-prescription cough medicine. Of course, any prescription medicines used on a regular basis, such as for allergies and other conditions, would likewise find space in your kit.

Prepare for these smaller medical inconveniences in advance. Closest friends and associates likely will murmur words of praise about you such as "genius," "gifted," and "outstanding" the first time they need a band-aid. Best of all, your mother will smile!

EMERGENCY

...for he [the Lord] guards the course of the just and protects the way of his faithful ones.

Proverbs 2:8

In battle after battle, the United States Army Rangers distinguished themselves with valor and success during World War II, often against seemingly impossible odds. Organized as a commando-type force under legendary Major (later General) William O. Darby, the Rangers adopted a novel organizational concept known as the "buddy system." No matter how large a Ranger unit might be, the unit based its training and operations on two-man teams chosen by the soldiers themselves. Why? Because good friends ("buddies") would work together better than non-friends. With a long history of success, the U.S. Army Rangers still use the buddy system today.

For a variety of good reasons, college students need a buddy system, too, particularly in times of medical emergency. Certainly we hope serious medical issues never arrive, but if they do, contingency plans for emergencies raise the likelihood of successful outcomes. First, you and a "buddy" (probably a roommate or someone living in close proximity) should share information about pertinent medical history, such as severe allergies, diabetes, seizures, and similar medical concerns, and whether medications may be required. Then, post each other's information in your room along with family phone numbers. Second, each of you needs to carry a medical insurance card. If you lack medical insurance, take a serious look at the student policies offered through colleges and universities; most are bargains. Third, take your "buddy" and visit the institution's infirmary (if one exists) and the nearest hospital. Quickly finding either facility during an emergency may mean the difference between life and death. (Note: some schools maintain strict policies governing medical emergencies and procedures for transporting injured or sick students, so ask about these to protect yourselves from potential liabilities.)

God represents the ultimate insurance policy, as noted by King Solomon. Still, you need to do your part, too. Find a buddy!

Unit Eight

Personality Primer

As a beginning college student, hundreds, if not thousands, of new faces share your college activities. Many of these new faces will become friends, and a smaller number will become close friends, some probably for life. What kind of image do you want to present to them? Think carefully about this before formulating an answer, because the answer contains lifelong implications. Consider for a moment that many of your friends will know you closely for four years or so, and then, most of them will disperse along paths separate from yours. Their image of you will come from memories, memories consisting of the person and behavior they witnessed in college.

Thus, how will your image appear to friends? Will friends remember you as the never-serious clown, the marginal student who always slept late, the party person who drank too much, the constant complainer, or the unreliable friend? In twenty or thirty years will you want to attend class reunions with people who remember these or other unflattering traits? Or, would you rather have people remember you as a person of character, a person on whom they could depend and trust? The choice belongs to you.

This unit will present a group of Scripturally-supported personality traits for your consideration. Look deep within yourself and ponder these personality traits; give an honest self-appraisal regarding their presence, or absence, in your personality. If any are lacking, with focus, determination, and prayer you can incorporate these desirable traits into your makeup. Remember, your life, image, and personality will become whatever you direct them to become. Choose well, and make a good impression on your college friends and associates.

CONSISTENT

The path of the righteous is like the first gleam of dawn, shining ever brighter till the full light of day.

Proverbs 4:18

Years ago in my boyhood, cowboy movies with their larger-than-life heroes completely captured my interest and imagination. These Saturday superstars (in white hats) who always vanquished the bad guys (in black hats) served as role models as I rode my imaginary horse across the "prairies" of our school playground. Not only could my heroes out-ride, out-shoot, and out-think the bad guys every time, but no Biblical character could equal them in moral virtue. Just imagine my dismay when later in life I attended a much-promoted baseball banquet and heard my favorite cowboy hero give a speech laced with profanity and dirty stories. Truthfully, the disappointment lingers with me today.

Christians sometimes lead double lives, too, and like my former cowboy hero, bring disappointment to the watching eyes of other people and God. Sadly, such people often do not perceive their own diminished stature among friends and peers; and, of course, any possible testimony of faith evaporates. Jesus labeled those with two-faced lives "hypocrites." Listen to this hard comment to hypocrites by Jesus: "on the outside you appear to people as righteous but on the inside you are full of hypocrisy and wickedness." (Matthew 23:28) Living a lie impresses no one!

Resolve now to let your path shine brighter every day, as King Solomon so beautifully described in today's Scripture verse. Although every Christian stumbles on the path sometimes, make clear in your own mind the intention to live a consistent life of faith--all the time. Friends and associates will respect your Christian character, and God will bless you. As a guiding statement for the Christian life, consider these insightful words from St. Francis of Assisi: "Preach the Gospel at all times and when necessary use words." Amen to consistent Christian living!

ENDURING

When the storm has swept by, the wicked are gone, but the righteous stand firm forever.

Proverbs 10:25

When hurricane Katrina unleashed its fury along the Gulf coast on August 29, 2005, the resulting devastation stunned a nation. The loss and disruption of human life, coupled with catastrophic property damage, rattled the political and social structure of the United States for a considerable time and forever changed our methods of responding to natural disasters. Yet, even with experience as our teacher, supported by great meteorological understanding, we cannot prevent these storms. More will come.

At a later time following Katrina, I journeyed to the Gulfport, Mississippi area with a local church group to rebuild a home for a low-income family devastated by the storm. As we surveyed the indescribable damage a few city blocks from the ocean, clearly the stronger houses had survived the storm with little damage, while the weaker houses crumbled. People often react to difficult situations in much the same way.

In life, as in nature, the storms will come. How individuals cope with difficult circumstances depends on a variety of variables, but God provides us with Scriptural ways of "stepping over" these variables and dealing directly with Him for endurance, or as we sometimes say, for "staying power." In Matthew 7:24 Jesus gave us an important principle: "Therefore, everyone who hears these words of mine and puts them into practice is like a wise man who built his house on the rock." Thus, Jesus tells all of us (students, too!) to study the Word in order to prepare for likely challenges in life. (As a practical matter, visit your local Christian bookstore and purchase a Bible study guide plus one of the many inexpensive collections of God's promises from Scripture. These types of materials help in focusing daily Bible study.)

College, with its many academic and social demands, often requires considerable staying power while working through stress-filled circumstances (which, by the way, serves as invaluable training for adulthood). How will friends see you during difficult times? Rely on God's Word for direction and endurance in standing through the storms.

COURAGEOUS

Have no fear of sudden disaster or of the ruin that overtakes the wicked, for the Lord will be your confidence....
Proverbs 3:25-26a

Chris Lofton, three-time basketball All-American and Southeastern Conference all-time three-point shot leader with 431 (wow!), appeared indomitable going into his senior season at the University of Tennessee. However, in reality, his senior season in 2007-08 did not go well. He seemed tired on the court, especially on defense, and his three-point shooting percentage fell noticeably. Press and fans alike wondered about Lofton and his "slump." Through it all, this great athlete made no excuses for his play; rather, he supported his team with hustle and encouragement. Following the season came a shocking revelation known only to his coach, family, and a few others close to the team: Chris Lofton had undergone treatment for testicular cancer in the spring of 2007, with a consequent loss of conditioning and strength for many months. What explanation did he give for not going public at the time? "I didn't want it to be a distraction for our team...." Immediately following the announcement, Lofton became a national hero, not for basketball, but for courage and unselfishness.

Courage comes in many forms, but it comes from the heart and not from some genetic quirk. Lofton, a Christian, gave credit to his Christian parents for supplying Bible verses and prayers to keep his faith strong through the painful ordeal of cancer. As Christians, we can work through Scripture and prayer to develop our courage for times of challenge. But in addition to a rock solid faith in God, courage requires personal determination, too. Listen to Chris Lofton again: "You're going to get knocked down. It's whether you stay down or whether you get back up and fight that counts." Yes!

Your need for courage may never occur with sports, or illness, or in any dramatic way. However, your call for courage may come in standing-up to everyday events, like "friends" who laugh at your Christian faith and challenge your beliefs, or who want your participation in unwise or immoral activities. As King Solomon advised, let the Lord become the confidence behind your courage. This kind of courage will stand!

HUMBLE

Humility and the fear of the Lord bring wealth and honor and life.
Proverbs 22:4

Pharaoh repeatedly displayed his arrogance and pride toward God despite numerous warnings from Moses. Unfortunately for Pharaoh, he did not comprehend how severely God despises arrogance. As a result, Pharaoh forfeited everything, including his life. Now, contrast Pharaoh with another Biblical person, Simeon, described as "righteous and devout" (Luke 2:25). Simeon, a humble man, walked with God's favor. Reflect upon the encounter at the temple when Simeon, guided by the Holy Spirit, recognized the baby Jesus as Messiah. Picture this man, probably trembling, as Mary and Joseph allowed him to hold the Son of God. Simeon then uttered one of the most beautiful tributes to God in all of Scripture (Luke 2:29-32). God blessed humble Simeon.

Both Old and New Testaments make it clear that God respects humility but dislikes a haughty attitude. Most Christian students seem to understand pride and arrogance on a heavenly level as rebellion against God; at the earthly level, almost everyone views pride and arrogance as obnoxious! On the other hand, confusion sometimes exists surrounding the definition of "humble." "Submissive to God" provides a good theological definition, but when speaking of friends "unassuming" and "not boastful" give us a broader picture of a humble person. We should never associate the concept of humility with weakness, as people sometimes do, because humble people may possess the strongest and most courageous of characters.

When friends think of you, now and in the future, what will they remember? Will they think of a self-centered person who constantly sought attention and praise at the expense of others, or will friends picture a generous person who promoted others? Humble or arrogant? The choice is yours, but choose wisely. One route leads to friendships and respect; the other does not.

RESPONSIBLE

Like a bad tooth or a lame foot is reliance on the unfaithful in times of trouble.
Proverbs 25:19

In the Civil War, the Battle of Gettysburg stands as a pivotal victory for the Union Army. Many historians view the outcome of the battle as a determining factor in the eventual defeat of the Confederacy. Within the overall Battle of Getttysburg, numerous smaller conflicts between armies raged in ferocious fighting. Little Round Top, a rocky hill on the extreme left flank of the Union Army, emerged as one such point of conflict on that day of July 2, 1863.

The Battle of Gettysburg might have been lost by the Union Army had it not been for the quick thinking of two Union officers. Brigadier General G.K. Warren, sent to survey the Union Army's left flank, found Little Round Top virtually undefended and badly exposing the entire battle force. Alarmed, Warren sent messengers seeking any available Union troops for defense of this hill. Another officer, Colonel Strong Vincent, hearing of the dilemma and without orders raced his four regiments to the hilltop with only ten minutes to spare before the battle began! Although Col. Vincent died in the fighting, his quick thinking, teamed with that of General Warren, saved the day at Little Round Top and perhaps even saved the Battle of Gettysburg for the Union.

In times of difficulty, we look for help from responsible people who can cope successfully with trouble. As King Solomon noted, undependable people offer little value in crisis. "Responsible" implies at least two qualities. First, as seen at Little Round Top, is a willingness to step forward and take charge. "Taking charge" may bring criticism after the crisis ends, often by those who second-guess from the sidelines. Second, "responsible" implies a readiness to stand behind one's actions without excuse or alibi. Blaming others for lack of successful outcomes offers simplicity but gains little respect.

Will friends and professors view you as unreliable under pressure, or will they see you as a person who shoulders responsibility with determination and creativity? Let daily faith see you through trials, that others might find you dependable. It's your responsibility!

FORGIVING

A man's wisdom gives him patience; it is his glory to overlook an offense.
Proverbs 19:11

Dag Hammarskjold, a Christian and second Secretary General of the United Nations, demonstrated extraordinary diplomatic skills and influence on the world stage during difficult years of the Cold War. Following his death by airplane crash in Africa in 1961, Hammarskjold received the Nobel Peace Prize. United States President John F. Kennedy referred to him as "the greatest statesman of our century." Intelligent and gifted in working with people of diverse cultures, Hammarskjold carried a reputation as a forgiving human being. Consider this quote from him:

> In the presence of God, nothing stands between Him and us-
> -we are forgiven. But we cannot feel His presence if anything
> is allowed to stand between ourselves and others.

Hammarskjold's statement closely mirrors the comments of Jesus in Matthew 18:35. Jesus bluntly told his disciples to forgive others in order to experience relationship with the Father. Why would Jesus make this terse comment? If we consider the parable preceding Jesus' statement, the reason confronts us clearly: God, through the sacrifice of Jesus, forgave our wrong-doings toward Him; in turn, we must grant forgiveness to those who hurt or mistreat us.

Of all human behavior, granting forgiveness seems the most difficult to do, perhaps because forgiveness means giving away our "right" to retaliation, or at least, to righteous indignation. Jesus said for us to forgive others an unlimited number of times. (Matthew 18:22) In other words, if we count the number of times we forgive, we likely have not forgiven at all!

Consider, too, that lack of forgiveness usually creates its own prison of bitterness and smoldering anger. Thus, an unforgiving person usually pays a personal price. Step to a higher level in the eyes of friends and God by forgiving others. You even may sleep better at night!

TRUTHFUL

The Lord detests lying lips, but he delights in men who are truthful.
Proverbs 12:22

Preceding the 2008 Beijing Olympic Games, expectations ran high for the United States track and field teams, particularly in the relay events. Loaded with top runners, the potential to win gold medals for both the women's and men's 4x100-meter relay teams made for on-going analysis and speculation by the media. But in the end neither relay team won gold. In fact, neither team competed in the gold medal event at all, because both had lost their preliminary qualifying races. How could such a shocking disappointment occur? Very easily. Amazingly, both teams violated the most basic assignment in running relays; both teams dropped the baton before reaching the finish line.

Just as dropping the baton caused these teams to lose their chance at winning a gold medal, failure to tell the truth--in other words lying-- will end your chances at making close friends faster than nearly any other act. "Trust" represents the most fragile of human instincts, and once broken, trust becomes difficult, if not impossible, to restore. Simply put, when direct lies, misleading statements, half-truths, gossip, or other false suggestions make their way into words, trust (and friendship) will break. Without naming names here, think of the prominent people including Presidents, congressional members, movie stars, and professional athletes, who lied publicly and then paid a severe price when the truth became known (as it usually does).

Not surprisingly, the Scriptures speak clearly and frequently about the importance of telling the truth. In fact, the subject of honesty in speech occurs far more frequently than some of the other commonly preached sins. King Solomon's words parallel those of both Old and New Testament writings, and the conclusion stands clearly: "The Lord detests lying lips...."

Remember, telling the truth never requires an apology; however, telling a lie often does. Gain the respect of others by becoming known as a person of your word, and watch your influence grow. Better still, God promises to bless you!

POSITIVE

He who pursues righteousness and love finds life, prosperity, and honor.
Proverbs 21:21

David, only a boy, accomplished one of the great feats of the Old Testament in slaying the giant Goliath with only a sling and a stone. For a display of courage and testimony to God, go to 1 Samuel 17 and read of this thrilling exploit by the young sheepherder who saved King Saul and Israel from the Philistines. As you read the Biblical account, look for something else in this story that may have escaped your notice previously. Look at David's attitude versus the attitudes of others and note the startling contrast. All of the army turned and ran from Goliath while the King lamented and tried to bribe someone--anyone--to fight Goliath. Worst of all, David's oldest brother, Eliab, grew angry and tried to send David home. The only positive person in the entire event, David, defied them all and went forward into battle.

David's story extends beyond mere positive thinking. The Scriptures tell about David's unshakable faith in God, the source of his positive attitude. In contrast, the cast of negative thinkers in the story seems to have forgotten all about God. From this, learn a valuable lesson about life. Negativity, an easy emotion, takes many forms, such as pessimism, blaming and criticizing others, and an absence of faith; further, negativity is widespread because it requires no courage or commitment to anything. As in the case of David, you will encounter negative people throughout life, people who will try to deflate your enthusiasm and discourage your ideas, sometimes quite forcefully. Just as David did, you must learn to ignore consistently negative people.

On the other hand, Christians should be the most positive people on earth, because God promised to inspire, lead, and protect us--and all of this in addition to our eternal salvation. Think of the influence you may have on others on a day-by-day basis. People will notice and appreciate your positive way of approaching life, and they will recognize in you the potential for success. Why? Because successful people nearly always display positive attitudes. Now, go slay some "giants."

DREAMER

There is surely a future hope for you, and your hope will not be cut off.
Proverbs 23:18

Kristi possesses a fierce determination about life, probably because life knocked her down several times. As a high school basketball player, her life became difficult when epilepsy appeared. Enduring excruciating headaches, seizures, and embarrassment, Kristi fought through these health issues and successfully played point guard on her high school team, while graduating as an honor student. Although playing basketball in college lost its appeal because of the epilepsy, she attended college via academic scholarship. The epilepsy intensified, and after long consideration, evaluation, and nonstop prayer, Kristi underwent dangerous, painful brain surgery at Johns Hopkins Hospital in hopes of correcting the problem. Through it all she never wavered from her dream of completing college. The result? Today Kristi, married and the proud holder of both undergraduate and graduate degrees, teaches math to high school students, a remarkable feat in light of the often debilitating effects of epilepsy, which prohibit the majority of epileptics from graduating college. How do I know so much about this story of a determined young woman pursuing her dreams against great odds? Kristi is our youngest child.

Chip Ingram, in his fine book *Good to Great in God's Eyes*[8], makes the following insightful statement:

> There is tremendous power in a dream. When you believe a picture of the future, and that bleeds out of your heart--not because you have to or ought to accomplish it, but because you intensely want to--it blows wind in your sails and directs the course of your life. It can also direct the course of history.

Everyone needs a dream, a passion, for purpose in living. Look deep inside and find yours. Then, ask yourself how much you are willing to sacrifice in order to make this dream happen. Although others may help and encourage along the way--such as the wonderful medical team at Johns Hopkins who aided Kristi--the determination to follow your dream must come from within. Be determined and confident, confident in King Solomon's assurance that God has a good future in store for you. What is your dream?

---

[8] Ingram, Chip. *Good to Great in God's Eyes.* Grand Rapids, MI: Baker Books, 2007. (Page 74)

MARATHONER

Make level paths for your feet and take only ways that are firm. Do not swerve to the right or the left; keep your foot from evil.
Proverbs 4:26-27

One of the great battles of human history took place between the Persians and Athenians on the plains of Marathon near Athens, Greece, in 490 B.C. History documents the battle and its outcome. However, less clearly recorded are details about a legendary character, Phidippides, whose fame grew from events surrounding the battle. Legend mixed with history contends that Phidippides, a soldier and professional runner, ran to Sparta and back (about 280 miles!) unsuccessfully seeking military help against the invading Persians. Then, after the vastly outnumbered Athenian army surprised and defeated the Persian army, Phidippides ran the news of victory to Athens twenty-six miles away. Following his announcement of victory, Phidippides promptly died. The Athenian victory prevented Persia from expanding its empire into Europe, and today Olympic marathons--always about twenty-six miles in length-- commemorate the heroic feat of Phidippides.

Like Phidippides and his "marathon," college, too, requires a long-distance run. Times and events of discouragement occur to all students. Whether the tough times come from disappointing grades, conflicts with friends, lack of career direction, or many other possibilities, successful students look beyond temporary setbacks toward correcting problem areas and accomplishing goals. Whatever the issues, take a proactive approach; in other words, do something positive to correct the problem. For example, if a grade is the issue, see the professor for corrective suggestions. Learn to look at the bigger picture, and never allow short-term problems to derail long-term goals.

Throughout this unit on "Personality Primer," we have discussed a number of desirable, Biblically-based personality traits for Christians. We can modify personality with conscious effort and God's help, and college provides a terrific opportunity for developing the "new" you. Just remember, college, like life, requires a long-distance perspective achieved on a daily basis.

Unit Nine

Relationship Roulette

Yes, the goal of "going to college" centers upon education and training for the future. Preparing for life as a wage-earning adult presumably convinced you, and probably your parents, to commit the money, time, and resources necessary for attending college. But let me share a truth at this point: some of your college relationships will outlast most of the knowledge you receive in college, because knowledge often changes with better understanding and research. In contrast, many of the friends and professional acquaintances made in college may endure for a lifetime.

In this unit we want to look at practical aspects of choosing different types of relationships in a college environment. For example, at a professional level relationships with professors, advisors, university administrators, administrative assistants, internship supervisors, and employers may not exist as close personal friendships, but these relationships often play a crucial role in a student's occupational future. On a social level, college offers wide opportunities for interaction through organizations such as fraternities, sororities, interest clubs, intramural sports, church-sponsored groups, and the like. From this group deep friendships often form. Finally, romantic relationships frequently develop in college, too, and we want to consider some timely thoughts for Christian students in this regard.

The goal of this unit focuses on choosing and nurturing positive relationships. Choosing relationships in college constitutes an important "non-credit" learning experience for every student. Some relationships will remain at a professional level, some will mature into close friendships, and some will assume great importance for the rest of your life. Learning to choose relationships carefully and wisely in college provides invaluable training for life.

VELCRO

He who walks with the wise grows wise, but a companion of fools suffers harm.

Proverbs 13:20

In 1948 following a hike, Swiss engineer George de Mestral studied the burrs taken from his pants and his dog's hair. Discovering tiny hooks on the ends of the burr spines prompted Mestral's follow-up invention of an artificial "burr" eventually named Velcro. Known for its ability to grip quickly and efficiently, Velcro today binds everything from children's shoes to astronaut gear.

Oftentimes, college students act as though Velcro binds them to their circle of friends. Sadly, these students seem bound to one another to the point of excluding other relationships. Particularly noticeable, students coming from the same hometown and high school frequently become cliquish. Certainly, possessing close friends from home or elsewhere can help in making the transition to college more pleasant. Yet, to hover with the same group most of the time eliminates one of the most significant aspects of college life, meaning, the development of new relationships. Among other things, these new relationships can provide insights into other cultures and viewpoints, can lead to new interests academically and socially, and can initiate life-long friendships, some of which may become valuable occupationally long after college graduation.

Because college generally requires most beginning students to start over in the relationship department, each student possesses a great opportunity for reaching out to others who likewise seek new relationships. Therefore, do not simply wait for new relationships eventually to take form; rather, be a little aggressive in taking the initiative to create introductions. In doing so, you will hone your social skills and lift your spirits at the same time. You may even provide happiness for someone else who needs a friend. Above all, ask God to provide guidance into relationships that He will bless. Then, as King Solomon noted, you will walk with the wise and grow wise.

DIAMOND MINDS

He who seeks good finds goodwill, but evil comes to him who searches for it.
Proverbs 11:27

To geologists, minerals represent a foundation for understanding the earth. Why? Briefly put, different minerals bound together by nature make rocks, and rocks make the geologic features seen across the earth. Amazingly, each mineral type possesses strict characteristics determined by nature's rules. For example, graphite (known to many as pencil "lead") feels slippery, is very soft, and will write on paper. But in the presence of great heat and pressure, graphite will rearrange its internal structure and become the hardest of natural substances, a diamond! It's true. The ugly duckling graphite can be turned into the most beautiful of minerals simply by following nature's rules.

Similarly, in developing relationships with new acquaintances, several "rules" should govern your approach. These simple rules may help create great friendships or they may help in avoiding great discomfort and disappointment. Consider the implications of these largely self-explanatory rules of relationship:

1. Friends do not require each other to change core values, like faith and morality. Failure here indicates a significant hurdle to close friendship.

2. Lasting friendships require effort and nurturing, even when offenses take place. Do you value each other enough to do this?

3. At any institution--public, private, or religious--whatever type of people you seek, you will find. Set high standards and look in the right places.

By this time you have begun to ask an important question: "Shouldn't I be friends with everyone?" Yes, of course you should. As Christians we should be friendly, kind, and respectful to everyone. However, close friends strike chords deep within us that may help or hurt, so exercise discretion. Draw a distinction between pleasant relationships and deep friendships. Both will be important to daily living, but only one will influence your life forever. Graphite or Diamonds?

LOYALTY LAPSE

A gossip betrays a confidence, but a trustworthy man keeps a secret.
Proverbs 11:13

Most of us likely would agree that trust and loyalty must exist in a friendship. The ability to rely on a friend's judgment and integrity give us confidence in sharing our hidden thoughts and experiences as well as our hopes and dreams. A friend would not divulge our privately shared comments with others--or would they? Sometimes, whether by accident or on purpose, we find breaches of our confidence by friends, and sometimes these breaches can be embarrassing, or worse.

In recent political history, perhaps no release of information by a "friend" carried repercussions to compare with the Monica Lewinsky scandal of 1997-99. Confiding in Linda Tripp, a co-worker and supposed friend, Monica Lewinsky shared the sordid details of an illicit sexual relationship with then President Bill Clinton. To Lewinsky's surprise and dismay, Ms. Tripp secretly recorded several incriminating telephone conversations and later shared them with others. The resulting investigation and political storm rocked the nation and contributed to the President's impeachment by the House of Representatives (the Senate acquitted Mr. Clinton). Aside from the obvious immorality and poor judgment by both Monica Lewinsky and Mr. Clinton, this scandal teaches a very clear lesson about sharing sensitive information with other people. Always exercise caution about what you say and to whom you say it.

Do the above ideas mean we should never share burdens, regrets, and other inmost thoughts with a trusted friend? No, but the example above (and many others) suggests using discretion in doing so. Even the best of friends may divulge secrets to others "who would never tell," and when this happens watch how fast the information circulates to wider and wider circles. Once again, King Solomon shared his practical insight about a serious issue. Loyalty lapses, intended or not, can hurt.

FRIENDS AND TSUNAMIS

A friend loves at all times....
Proverbs 17:17a

The most destructive tsunamis, or seismic sea wave, in modern history struck on December 26, 2004 in the Indian Ocean. Generated by a tremendous earthquake (9.3 on the Richter Scale) near the coast of Sumatra, Indonesia, the tsunamis raced across the Indian Ocean creating massive devastation and death along shore areas in places as far away as eastern Africa. Imagine this terrifying ocean wave moving nearly 500 miles per hour and slamming into populated coastal areas. In the aftermath of this horrific event, a minimum of 250,000 people had died, and the dollar costs ranged in the billions.

Like the tsunamis, life sometimes places unavoidable difficulties in our path, and we may not see the difficulty approaching until it slams us. The telephone call came around 5:00 in the morning: Luke (our seven year-old grandson) could not stand, speak, or walk properly. Two days later after tests at Johns Hopkins Hospital, further bad news arrived. Luke's problems were originating from an inoperable malignant brain tumor. Our "tsunamis" had hit. Throughout the ordeal of treatments, anxiety, sorrow, and pain, many thoughtful and wonderful displays of compassionate friendship from a variety of sources came to our family. Yet, none was more supportive and comforting than the encouragement offered to Lisa, Luke's mother, by her dear friend and former college roommate. Special friends count in times of trouble.

During your days in college, stay mindful of the value of close friends. We all need them. Ultimately, the key to making close friends comes down, not to the question "Can I make friends?," but to "Can I be a friend?" Value highly your college friends. My mother-in-law still communicated regularly with her former roommate and best friend--and both of them were ninety years young!

GOING PRO

The wisdom of the prudent is to give thought to their ways....
Proverbs 14:8a

Nurses enable healthcare in America to function at high efficiency levels. As a former board member of two different hospitals in our area, I learned long ago of the profound medical service performed by registered nurses ("RN's"); in fact, without nurses healthcare in America would grind to a halt. Possessing a powerful blend of intelligence and compassion, nurses usually display a level of professionalism seldom seen in other occupations. Much of this professionalism originates in student training. From the beginning, nursing students learn professional standards and develop professional relationships with their mentors. Thus, by graduation professionalism defines their outlook.

Most students outside of nursing (and a very few other fields), rarely appear to give professionalism much thought, at least until looking for a job after graduation. How can a student start preparing professionally? First, understand that course work and credits, while extremely important, do not provide complete preparation for professional life. Second, develop professional relationships. These relationships often quietly teach much about the profession not included in textbooks, such as what to say or not to say and how to dress appropriately. Further, these relationships may prove invaluable after graduation for job contacts and recommendations.

Professional relationships should begin for most students with professors and college administrators in the likely field of study. Make a point of attending departmental seminars, presentations, or social functions and introducing yourself to appropriate individuals. After a few times, these individuals will recognize your ongoing interest. In addition, you may possess other opportunities to develop professional relationships through internships, work-study for the department, field trips, and the like. Always look at the bigger picture of becoming a professional. In other words, think like a nurse!

COWBOYS AND PROFESSORS

...preserve sound judgment and discernment, do not let them out of your sight; they will be life for you, an ornament to grace your neck.
Proverbs 3:21-22

Perhaps you know the old story of the cowboy who, when seeing a railroad train chugging across the plains for the first time, immediately spurred his horse into a gallop, whirled his lasso, and tried to rope the locomotive--all to an unfortunate end for him and the horse. Onlookers were said to praise loudly the cowboy's courage but to express serious reservations about his judgment! Well, as strange as things may seem, students sometimes seem determined to "lasso trains" when it comes to making good impressions on their professors.

Because of classroom interaction, professors quite naturally form the first level of professional relationships available to college students. However, many students fail to connect positively with their professors, either by timidity or neglect; and some students simply create poor impressions when interaction does take place. For example, poor classroom performance, absences, rude behavior, and regularly slovenly appearance produce negative images. Further, some students mistakenly try to establish friendships with professors, rather than professional relationships. Most wise professors strive to maintain a social distance from students. Instead of friendship, most professors prefer an amiable but professional relationship. Put yourself in the professor's place: showing close friendship with a student inevitably looks like favoritism to other students and unfairly characterizes the professor. As a student, show enthusiasm and interest for the course and profession, but at the same time respect the social boundaries.

Why should students care about the impressions made with their professors, aside from grades? Most professors possess many contacts in the professional world, and at a future time you likely will ask some of them for introductions and recommendations for jobs or graduate school. Their recommendations can make a significant impact in your life. Learn with King Solomon to "preserve sound judgment and discernment...." as you interact with professors. No more lassos!

SPIRITUAL WAVELENGTHS

Through love and faithfulness sin is atoned for; through the fear of the Lord a man avoids evil.

Proverbs 16:6

In these days of energy awareness, solar energy provokes great interest as a "green" energy source. After all, solar energy arrives every day free of charge! My fascination with solar energy came years ago while taking several graduate classes in meteorology. (I know, I lead a dull life.) In any case, solar energy lacks uniformity as it zooms through space as waves of energy. For example, some potentially damaging waves like gamma rays and x-rays are unimaginably short. Others like infrared are very long and travel at the opposite end of the wavelength spectrum. Visible light falls between very long and very short waves. Why care about solar wavelengths? For one thing, life on earth depends upon them for survival.

Likewise for Christians, spiritual "wavelengths" often determine the life of relationships, especially romantic ones. As such, "being on the same wavelength," meaning spiritual compatibility, should constitute the chief concern of every Christian entering a romantic relationship. The Apostle Paul said this: "Do not be yoked together with unbelievers" (2 Corinthians 6:14a). Paul goes on to explain the total spiritual incompatibility between a believer and a non-believer. Although restricting yourself to dates with Christians may seem a lonely or difficult path, doing so promises God-inspired results.

Look and pray for Christians to date. As you learn more about each new person, ask yourself some critical questions. "Does this person value spirituality and put it into action each day?" "Do the Christian values of this person come close to mine?" "Does this person 'walk the walk' regardless of situation or consequences?" Deal intelligently with emerging romantic relationships by looking honestly at spiritual compatibility. Remember the importance of those spiritual wavelengths.

JUST WORDS?

Pleasant words are a honeycomb, sweet to the soul and healing to the bones.

Proverbs 16:24

Words portray the character of culture. Some words tie us to the past, such as "patriotism," "forefathers," and "childhood." Other words tell us of dynamic changes in society. Words like "e-mail," "internet," and "smart phone" did not exist a few years ago; however, today these words occupy a part of nearly everyone's vocabulary. Churches change, too, and along with change comes new terminology. Many older people remember worshipping each Sunday in a "sanctuary." Today a "worship center" stands there, and a "praise team" may sing in place of a choir. Whatever the change--social, technological, or religious--words reflect our cultural status.

Not surprisingly, then, words can tell us a lot about the status of a romantic relationship. Think honestly. What words come to mind in describing the relationship and the person romantically close to you, or perhaps someone you would like to date? Do the words reflect positive values and emotions, or in contrast, do the words indicate negative feelings? No healthy relationship carries significant negative baggage for very long and survives. Christians need relationships with other positive Christians in order for dating to be both fun and enriching. To accept less in a romantic relationship risks masking serious differences which will surface later, especially in marriage.

Finally, as in other relationships, the people you date will reflect your character; by association friends and colleagues will draw conclusions about your moral convictions. What image do you wish to portray to friends? Take the high road by living your faith while dating. After developing the word lists described in the preceding paragraph, exercise discernment in your choices. After all, romantic relationships consist of more than just words!

RIGHT PLACE, RIGHT TIME

A longing fulfilled is sweet to the soul....
Proverbs 13:19a

As the small airplane circled lazily over the mountains of eastern Tennessee, the pilot, a music minister and friend of my father, asked an unexpected question: "Since our church is without a pastor, would you lead our mid-week service tonight?" Inwardly I grimaced and thought of all the reasons I should not do this. My limited time frame for researching a masters degree thesis from Michigan State University, my lack of preparation for the church service just three hours away, and my inexperience in the pulpit all shouted "No!" However, John had been a life-saver in volunteering to provide introductions to key people and a birds-eye view of my thesis study area. "John," I said with forced enthusiasm, "I would be happy to lead the service."

While surveying the small Wednesday night audience before speaking, my eyes locked onto a beautiful young lady sitting with her mother near the back of the room. Taking my eyes from her required great effort, and I did not do it often. Eventually I finished the meager message, the service ended, and church members came forward to greet and shake hands. As she--I did not know her name--touched my hand and looked at me, I believe at that moment we both knew we belonged to one another. Engaged and married within the year, Sylvia has been my wife and best friend for over forty years.

Romantic relationships do not occur as often as other types of relationships, but they require more discernment, emotional energy, and nurturing than all the rest combined. For Christians, prayer stands as the single most important act surrounding the relationship. In my case, I prayed diligently for six years for God's leadership in finding His choice of a wife for me; but even though I dated frequently, relationships failed the "rightness" test. Loneliness hurts, and at times I felt overlooked by God. Then, on God's timetable and at the least expected moment, Sylvia and I met and we knew. Imagine the result if I had refused to lead the service that night. I would have missed God's plan for my life and Sylvia's. Put yourself in the right places, and God will handle the right time.

ULTIMATE RELATIONSHIP

I love those who love me, and those who seek me find me.
Proverbs 8:17

The story of Naaman (2 Kings 5) provides insight into the mind of God regarding relationships with Him. A powerful man politically, Naaman commanded the army for the king of Aram, a country near Israel. Brave and militarily successful, Naaman feared nothing, except the leprosy carried in his body. At the suggestion of a servant girl, Naaman went to Israel where he encountered the prophet Elisha, who instructed Naaman to bathe seven times in the muddy Jordan River for healing. Do you remember Naaman's reaction? Rage! Rage at God's way of doing things, and Naaman went away, still unclean with leprosy. Eventually listening to the pleas of his servants, Naaman went to the Jordan, followed God's command, and experienced instant healing. Naaman responded with one of the great confessions in all of history: "Now I know that there is no God in all the world except in Israel." (v. 15)

God wants relationship with every person; but God, as in the case of Naaman, prescribed a process for relationship. Every person must follow this process by voicing repentance for sin, asking God's forgiveness, and confessing Jesus Christ as Lord. Now, compare God's way with popular opinion. A recent poll by ABC News found that ninety percent of Catholics, eighty-one percent of non-evangelical protestants, and forty-one percent of evangelical protestants in America believe that Christians *and* non-Christians will live in heaven after death. Wow! This may embody political correctness, but not theological correctness. God's Word tells of only one way, through Jesus.

God invites everyone to join in the ultimate relationship, a relationship with Him. Doing so bonds a person not only to God, but to all other followers of Christ as well. Just think, by an act of confession to God, we then enjoy relationship with God and with Christians around the world. As the bumper sticker says, "the benefits are out of this world."

Unit Ten

Faith Anchors

In previous units our goals focused mostly upon problems encountered by students transitioning from high school into college life. In other words, concerns of a practical nature dominated our attention. "Faith Anchors" maintains the practical theme of our book, but the direction shifts from every day student concerns to spiritual issues which can strengthen, or undermine, our faith. Thus, on a life basis the considerations discussed in this unit become some of the most important issues of all.

Going to college and maturing into adulthood prepares students for leadership roles in society. Many personal concepts about the world, our nation, and God will take form during the college years, even though these eventually may change with time and experience. What kind of person will emerge at the end of your college tunnel? A person of confident faith? A person without any faith other than human reason? Does spiritual growth rank as highly as intellectual growth in your college plan? The answer to this last question tells us much about the person who likely will appear at college graduation. College can provide a wonderfully liberating environment, but college likewise can insist upon rather rigid ways of thinking, particularly in areas of morality, social change, and spirituality. Who will you become?

The purpose of Unit Ten centers upon the spiritual measures of personal growth during college and offers concrete supports ("anchors") of faith. Challenges to faith--some direct, some subtle--nearly always arise in a scholarly environment. Let's look at how to prepare for these inevitable challenges.

WHERE?

He who fears the Lord has a secure fortress, and for his children it will be a refuge.

Proverbs 14:26

Abram demonstrated great obedience to God on numerous occasions, but never more so than when God commanded him to move his family to Canaan. Try to picture the broader setting for God's call to Abram. Living in Haran (located in northern Mesopotamia in today's northern Syria), Abram possessed family and wealth. Surrounded by friends and perhaps family who worshipped other gods, this seventy-five year-old man remarkably sensed God's hand upon his life. (Remember, Abram could not rely upon God's written Word because it did not exist at that time.) Thus, when God commanded a move to Canaan, Abram listened and acted. (See Genesis 12 for the complete story.)

Each time I read this story, I wonder how family and friends reacted when Abram told them of the up-coming journey to their new home in a far-off land. I can almost hear them asking in chorus: "Where?" Yet acting on faith, Abram left his home for Canaan and received God's blessings in the process.

As a student experiencing the nearly continuous clutter and pressure of college life, learn to hear the calm, quiet voice of God speaking to you. His message may arrive through a "tug" or an inclination, other people's experience, studying the Word, or in a hundred other ways. God speaks, but do we always listen and hear? One of your strongest anchors in times of disappointment, loneliness, decision-making, or other important emotional events consists of talking and listening to God for direction. Thus, cultivate your listening skills through regular quiet time and prayer.

As God leads your life in paths not anticipated by close friends and family, mentally and spiritually prepare for questions and perhaps disagreement from them. The doubters cannot know of God's will and direction in your life, at least until discussion occurs. Even then, sometimes our plans must reflect our faith rather than a desire to please those around us. When God speaks, an attitude of "anywhere" pleases Him. Asking "where?" likely does not.

OPEN THE BOOK

Fear God and keep his commandments, for this is the whole duty of man.
Ecclesiastes 12:13

As a boy, reading the Scriptures became a nightly event before bedtime. I rarely remembered much of the readings, for I often fell asleep as I read; however, I almost never missed a night. Why? Our church required every Sunday School member to record our progress on the "Five Point Record System" form each week. Of the required categories, "daily Bible reading" needed a check mark in order to receive a 100% score, and in our home, anything less than 100% brought parental review!

Now, contrast my childhood interest in Scripture with the Jews who had returned from many years of exile in Babylon. Because of sins against God, the beloved city of Jerusalem lay ruined from its destruction in 586 B.C. Under the leadership of Nehemiah, rebuilding of the city wall reached completion in 445 B.C. Soon afterward, all the people gathered within the walls as Ezra, the priest, stood high on a platform above the people and opened the Book of the Law. Ezra read aloud the Word of God to the people from daybreak until noon. How did the people respond? For hours in the baking sun, hands raised, people bowed, "Amen" sounded, and the people wept for joy in hearing God's Word. Through reading of the Word, revival came to Jerusalem!

Now, show some honesty with yourself. Do the Scriptures make any difference in your life? Do you seriously study the Scriptures looking for answers and insights into the mind and will of God? If not, why not? Think for a moment about the drama of the Scriptures, in that God took the time to reveal Himself to us through them. In times of academic challenge to your beliefs, in times of difficulty, and in times of joy the Scriptures allow us to tap into the wisdom of God. But interpreting God's Word never comes randomly. Rather, as missionary friends constantly remind me, we need to live "in the Word" with frequent study.

I believe Ezra would say, "Open the Book!"

SPIRITUAL CUBES

For whoever finds me [wisdom] finds life and receives favor from the Lord.
Proverbs 8:35

In ancient times, table salt held great value. In fact, Roman soldiers frequently received their salary in salt. Perhaps we take salt for granted, but chemically this common substance displays remarkable traits. For example, individually the two elements making up salt, sodium and chlorine, damage living tissue; but joined together the two elements produce a tasty mineral worthy of all the world's french fries! Further, if with magic glasses you could look inside a grain of salt, you would see a hidden universe of tiny cubes stacked neatly together, each cube consisting of four sodium and four chlorine atoms. Just how many of these invisible cubes does it take to build a grain of salt? It takes an incredible 56×10^{17} cubes. Amazing, isn't it? If those tiny cubes came in dollars you could buy the world, with money left over!

Spiritual growth in some ways resembles the grain of salt, because many small, invisible insights must come together in order to build a mind for God. Nature builds a grain of salt by adding the tiny, invisible cubes one at a time until the number of cubes becomes so great we begin to see the grain of salt. Likewise, God builds a spiritual mind by adding pieces of understanding one at a time until a Godly spirit becomes visible. But spiritual growth does not occur automatically. Enlarging our understanding of God requires studying Scripture, praying, worshipping, and serving on a regular basis.

Nearly every student grapples with time management in college. Still, everyone wanting relationship with God and spiritual growth must schedule time for Bible study and prayer each day. Look for supportive Christian friends and a church with people who will help you grow. God will place the "spiritual cubes" in the right order, but you must be willing to help in creating them. As King Solomon urged, find life in God's wisdom. In other words, seek and grow spiritually.

KNEE-DEEP IN BARLEY

As water reflects a face, so a man's heart reflects the man.

Proverbs 27:19

Eleazar, friend of King David, shines in his brief mention in the Bible. In fact, 1 Chronicles 11:12 describes him as "one of the three mighty men..." of David. The reason for this fearless reputation shows readily in verses 13-14. David's army, standing in a field of barley, faced the wicked and dreaded Philistine army. The Scripture recounts a full scale "panic attack" as the Israelites turned and fled--except for David and Eleazar. We will never know if these two warriors had second thoughts about their choice of activities for the day, but the Bible tells us they took their stand in the middle of the barley field against the Philistine army. Here we need to mention how God plus two men made a majority, because these two men of God "struck the Philistines down, and the Lord brought about a great victory!" God respects and uses humans with courageous hearts.

Not everyone encounters a need for physical bravery like Eleazar and David. But at some point--probably many points--everyone receives a challenge "to stand in the barley field" as a Godly person and confront unacceptable issues or actions by others. Although Christians must always treat other people respectfully, sometimes the situation calls for firmness and determination. Do you possess this type of courage? Many people do not. A young college student once made the following useful observation: "God does not give us courage; rather, God presents us with opportunities to demonstrate courage." Again, are you willing to show your courage on God's behalf?

As a college student, intellectual challenges to your faith likely will occur. View these encounters as opportunities to share with others and as opportunities for personal growth. No, you probably will not win all of the discussions, but if you participate, your skills in presenting beliefs, defending against competing ideas, and influencing others will improve steadily.

Standing up to challenges requires preparation, faith, and courage. Look deeply. What kind of person does your heart reflect?

UPRIGHT PRAYER

The Lord detests the sacrifice of the wicked, but the prayer of the upright pleases him.

Proverbs 15:8

When I read of great prehistoric structures in the world, I wonder. I wonder about the ancient people who built them, and just why they took the time and effort to do so. Too, I wonder what part religion played in prompting these significant engineering projects. For example, England's Stonehenge, in spite of intense study, remains largely a mystery. Did the people design it as a giant solar "calendar," a place of healing, a place important to their religious beliefs, or something else? Numerous theories claim adherents, but truthfully, scholars do not know for certain. Similar types of questions apply to other famous places such as Machu Picchu, Peru, the famous "Lost City of the Incas," and "The Great Pyramid of Cholula," important to the Aztecs of central Mexico.

In these and many other prehistoric sites, religion in many forms permeated life. It seems all people everywhere possess a desire to worship something or someone. The Apostle Paul tells us in Romans 1 and 5 how God revealed himself, in a limited way, to humans before the Law of Moses and Scripture. Briefly stated, then as now people could choose to worship God or refuse to do so. Placing myself in their place, I try to imagine "experiencing God" without benefit of Scripture and formal knowledge of prayer. Each time, I come away grateful for the revelations from Scripture, Christian family, experiences of other Christians, and prayer.

Prayer serves as our direct link to God. As a college student, prayer gives daily connection for many things touched upon in some of our previous devotional thoughts. Although prayer can take many forms, access to God through prayer in *any* form constitutes a precious gift to us. God promises to listen to the prayers of the "upright"; thus, Christians need to exercise the privilege of prayer regularly. This "anchor" steadies many aspects of faith as we speak and listen to the Creator. Use prayer often and wisely. God listens.

RICOCHET PRAYERS

All a man's ways seem right to him, but the Lord weighs the heart.
Proverbs 21:2

Beautiful places and fly-fishing for trout seem to go together. Trekking high in the Rocky Mountains each summer, fly rod in hand, provides soul-stirring memories for me of the Creator's handiwork, as does wading a Smoky Mountain stream amid the gorgeous colors of a fall day. All told, few activities match the timeless serenity of "presenting" artificial dry flies to trout--that is, most of the time. Occasionally, even in magnificent settings, nature presents obstacles to the trout fisherman. For example, sunlight bouncing off of the water's mirror-like surface can render a fly invisible to the angler (in fly fishing, the fisherman needs to see the artificial fly on the water). Fortunately, good sunglasses usually solve much of the problem.

Sometimes our prayer life may resemble sunlight bouncing from the water, in that, no matter how much or how hard we pray, the prayers seem to ricochet from the surrounding ceiling and walls. In other words, our prayers do not seem to leave the room where we are. "Ricochet prayers" yield frustration, and invariably we ask, "What's wrong?" No simple or single answer solves the problem (like sunglasses for fishing a trout stream), but we can observe two Biblical truths. For one, this is not a God problem; God in His unchanging manner listens to the prayers of believers. Secondly, the problem stems from within us and requires correction in order for God to acknowledge our prayers (see Matthew 5:21-26). Prayer demands openness before God; openness requires correcting any problems standing between us and God.

What issues may stand between God and an individual? The list includes many possibilities. Violation of God's commandments, mistreatment of other people, failure to stand upon Biblical principles in daily life, and the list goes on. Mostly, God wants us to possess a perfect heart, a heart at peace with people around us and with Him. Resolve the heart issues first; meaningful prayer will follow.

TAKE A WALK

I was appointed from eternity, from the beginning, before the world began.
Proverbs 8:23

Someday in heaven, I hope to meet Enoch and the Apostle Paul. Enoch intrigues me, because before written Scriptures existed and before Abraham received his marching orders as patriarch of God's chosen nation, Enoch became known for his faith in God. In fact, Genesis 5:22 says, "Enoch walked with God...." Now, fast forward to the New Testament and read of Paul--brilliant, fearless, and on a mission. As a college professor, one of my favorite passages of Scripture focuses upon Paul's engaging the Athenians in debate (Acts 17:16-34). Athens, Greece, a center of learning in Paul's day, highly valued debate and reason much like universities today. Imagine this feisty Jew, standing before a crowd of scholars boldly presenting the Gospel of Jesus to the best philosophical minds of the day. I would like to have been in the audience!

Both of these men walked with God along paths of faith, but their "jobs" took them in different directions of service. Enoch, for his great faith, escaped death and went directly to heaven (Hebrews 11:5). Whereas, Paul suffered beatings, prison confinement, verbal abuse, and finally execution while becoming the great missionary of the New Testament. Although God led these men of faith along different paths, in heaven both stand equally tall in God's evaluation. Walking with God yields its benefits!

As a college student, many choices and decisions await you in the coming four years, and in previous devotions we dealt with many of these. However, the most significant choice will pertain to walking with God throughout your college experience. Will an unshakable faith serve as your foundation for living, or will every new idea and theory bring doubts about God? When all else fails, remember the Scripture above. God existed before time or creation, and He is big enough to handle any idea or theory found in a college classroom. Should doubts arise, remember Enoch and Paul. They walked with God. What will heaven's ledger say about you?

WILLING HANDS

Do not withhold good from those who deserve it, when it is within your power to act.

Proverbs 3:27

Churches and houses built by volunteers from the First Baptist Church of Kingston, Tennessee, stand in numerous communities in the eastern United States. Long ago this church followed God's leadership into a building ministry for poor or small congregations and for families who could not afford the labor and related costs of new structures. From Habitat for Humanity houses in Tennessee, to homes for the devastated poor following Hurricane Katrina, to churches in Missouri, Michigan, and Maryland and most of the states in between, this congregation repeatedly opens their hearts, hands, and pocketbooks to help those in need.

Perhaps the most remarkable aspect of all regarding this building ministry relates to the group itself. Of the fifty or sixty men and women who participate, only five or six know much about construction or can read a blueprint; the remainder, as the construction leader of the group once told me, "simply offer willing hands." Visit a building site and you will observe men, women, and young people from all walks of life lifting, carrying, sweeping, and hammering. No heroes or stars exist, only "willing hands" under supervision of the few who know construction. But astounding results regularly occur in the form of buildings, encouraged congregations, and renewed hope for families, each an answer to intense prayer by the group before, during, and after a project.

What will characterize your college life? Will classmates remember you as considerate and helpful toward others, or will your time in college consist of an inward focus on personal goals? Think hard about your answer, because your life in college may become a preview of the rest of your life. If you are not willing to make a few sacrifices now for worthy projects, will the future be any different? Simply put, will your hands be closed fists asking, "What's in it for me?" Or like the Kingston builders, will you present open, "willing hands" to help others?

BREVITY

Let love and faithfulness never leave you; bind them around your neck, write them on the tablet of your heart. Then you will win favor and a good name in the sight of God and man.

Proverbs 3:3-4

While touring Europe with thirty-five high school students, our group visited Zermatt, a small Swiss village recognized mostly by mountain climbers and geography teachers. My adrenaline flowed vigorously at the thought of Zermatt. Why the enthusiasm? For years I had taught students about the geographical and geological significance of the Matterhorn, the spectacular mountain of the Alps, but my teaching originated from textbooks. Now, a few miles from town by train, I would visit the majestic mountain.

Unexpectedly, a strange event on the way to the Matterhorn changed my perspective. As we strolled toward the train station, the route led through a large, beautifully kept cemetery in the village. In reading the headstones, we noticed the large number, probably a majority, of young and middle-aged persons; and then we noticed how most had died--they had died trying to climb the beautiful, but deadly, mountain. Somberly, each gravestone posted some of the mountain-climbing gear of the fallen climber. The message of death to those so young seemed to override the mountain's splendor.

Life presents many wonderful possibilities for enjoyment and fulfillment, but nowhere do we find a guarantee regarding length of life. (Remember, not one of the mountain climbers in the Zermatt cemetery planned to die on the Matterhorn.) Rather, we should seek to make the most of each day. The Bible put it like this in Ephesians 5:15-16a: "Be very careful, then, how you live--not as unwise but wise, making the most of every opportunity...." Enjoy life but live it with purpose, for even a brief life can yield significant results.

How do we live wisely? First and foremost seek God's will each day. At the same time, apply King Solomon's poetic command by writing love and faithfulness "on the tablet of your heart." Solomon tells us that in doing so we will gain favor with God and those around us. Is not this outcome the greatest of compliments? Is not this the way to lead our nation back into God's design? Climb the right mountain.

ONE NATION

Righteousness exalts a nation, but sin is a disgrace to any people.
Proverbs 14:34

The United States stands on the precipice of great moral and social change. To be sure, we should encourage change which results in fair treatment for all members of the nation. Fair treatment reflects God's love for all people and builds national unity. However, increasingly in the discussion of "change" we see a dismissal of God. In fact, national leaders and the media rarely, if ever, refer to God. The usual reasons center upon political and social correctness for fear of offending those who follow other, or no, religious beliefs. As popular as this reasoning may be with our leaders, Scripture and history tell us of God's total rejection of the idea, and both Scripture and history show a trail of destroyed nations who tried ignoring God.

Actually, the path to successful nationhood is amazingly straightforward, perhaps even simple in concept. Listen to the words of Chronicles 7:14.

> If my people, who are called by my name, will humble themselves and pray and seek my face and turn from their wicked ways, then will I hear from heaven and will forgive their sin and will heal their land.

This promise from God our forefathers took seriously. Our constitution and legal system found their roots and substance in Scripture, and our leaders openly sought and acknowledged God's leadership. Because of faith and God's blessing, America became the most successful and generous nation in the world, standing its ground against evil through numerous wars and challenges. Now some want "change" away from God.

Your generation at some point will furnish the business, political, and social leadership for this nation. What contribution will you make? College provides great opportunities for developing leadership skills and formulating ideas regarding the future. More than ever, this nation needs knowledgeable, perceptive Christians in leadership roles. Perhaps "change" for your generation will mean leading the nation back to God.

Epilogue

Professors usually try to put in the last word. I shall maintain this fine tradition as a means of completing one of the goals of this book which, to repeat, was to present a clear process for Christian students in dealing with life's problems, whether in college or later in life. The design of nearly all of the book's devotional topics follows a pattern shown in the acrostic "P.R.A.Y."

        P. Pray constantly for understanding after identifying the problem.

        R. Read the Scriptures.

        A. Analyze the problem in the light of prayer and Scripture.

        Y. Yield to God's leadership in the matter.

Thus, the process is a simple one. Just remember to "P.R.A.Y." about each of life's problems! God will hear and help, if you do your part.

Thank you for permitting me to serve as your "professor" by way of this book. I wish you the very best of success and God's blessings as you proceed through college.

Author's Note

When God planted the seed in my mind and the burden on my heart to write this book, little did I realize that the experience would hearken back to my baseball days when the success of the pitcher was equally dependent on a willingness of teammates to contribute to the overall goal of accomplishing the task at hand. Of course, in baseball the goal was to win. With this book, the goal was simply follow God's call to minister to college students. However, I would like to thank my team members in this endeavor: my wife and best friend, Sylvia Charton, for being a sounding board and my first editor; and my daughter, Katie Charton Manning, for her editorial assistance. I would also like to thank my daughter, Kristi Charton Turner, and my son-in-law, Eric Manning, for their technical support in this venture.

41249993R00074

Made in the USA
Lexington, KY
05 May 2015